People Skills for Young Adults

Márianna Csóti

Jessica Kingsley Publishers
London and Philadelphia

First published in the United Kingdom in 2000 by
Jessica Kingsley Publishers
116 Pentonville Road
London N1 9JB, UK
and
400 Market Street, Suite 400
Philadelphia PA 19106, USA.

www.jkp.com

© Copyright 2000 Márianna Csóti
Second impression 2001
Printed digitally since 2004

Library of Congress Cataloging in Publication Data

Csóti, Márianna, People skills for young adults / Márianna Csóti. p. cm.
Includes bibliographical references and index.
ISBN 1 85302 716 2 (pb: alk paper_
1. Young adults--United States--Psychology. 2. Young adults--United States--Life skills guides. 3. Self-esteem in young adults--United States. 4. Social skills--United States.
1. Title. HQ799.7.C76   1999   98--45887
306'.14'0835--dc21   CIP

British Library Cataloguing in Publication Data

Csóti, Márianna,
People skills for young adults
1. Social skills – Study and teaching – Great Britain 2. Learning disabled youth – Education – Great Britain I. Title
302'.087

ISBN 1 85302 716 2

£17.95

People Skills for Young Adults

of related interest

Social Awareness Skills for Children
Marianna Csoti
ISBN 1 84310 003 7

The Social Skills Game
Yvonne Searle and Isabelle Streng
ISBN 1 85302 336 1

Incorporating Social Goals in the Classroom
A Guide for Teachers and Parents of Children with
High-Functioning Autism and Asperger Syndrome
Rebecca A. Moyes
ISBN 1 85302 967 X

Nonverbal Learning Disabilities at Home
A Parent's Guide
Pamela B. Tanguay
ISBN 1 85302 940 8

Pretending to be Normal
Living with Asperger's Syndrome
Liane Holliday Willey
ISBN 1 85302 749 9

Asperger's Syndrome
A Guide for Parents and Professionals
Tony Attwood
ISBN 1 85302 577 1

Contents

Part 3

About the Course

This book is divided into three parts. Part One concentrates on friendships: why we need them and the benefits gained from being in a supportive social network; sex differences between friendships; how our personal development has been affected by the relationships we have had; why people become lonely; the development of friendships – the process of making friends and what determines how intimate a relationship becomes or whether a budding friendship fails.

Part Two concentrates on the social (interpersonal) skills between two people and the skills needed in developing relationships: body language; the different types of social inadequacies with relevant role plays; hidden messages; the importance of appropriate self-disclosure; listening skills; overcoming shyness and making conversation in a variety of social interactions. Social rules are considered and their purpose.

Part Three deals with assertiveness and counselling skills (in an informal setting – that is, peer counselling rather than professional counselling). Both the assertiveness skills and counselling skills are techniques for 'fine tuning' relationships, going that step further to reach more meaningful levels of communication and satisfaction within relationships, learning how to verbally protect oneself and help friends and acquaintances find their own solutions to problems.

Leader's Notes

Social skills are essential life-skills. Knowledge of how relationships are formed aid self-awareness of what we do right and what we do wrong with certain people. A large element of social or 'people' skills is involved with communication and much of this course requires students to take part in discussion which aids their communication skills. The leader or teacher needs to be sensitive to students' feelings since many may have poor social skills and few friends, although the course will be of general benefit and is not aimed at just those who experience social distress. Jokes must not be made at the expense of some students less fortunate in their skills at handling social interactions.

The intended length of each session is one hour.

The course has been written with the intention that no research or preparatory work is required by the leader other than reading the material before the session and occasionally planning a session ahead so that students come prepared with, for example, certain role play ideas.

The ideas suggested in the leader sheets are by no means prescriptive or fully comprehensive. Students may well have other, or more, ideas relating to their own experiences. Similarly, any solutions given may have excellent alternatives that are equally or more valid. The aims of giving these solutions are to save preparation time, to give full understanding to the leader of what is required from the tasks set and to present as much assistance as possible for the session to progress smoothly. The leader sheets are not intended for student use, but to guide the leader. At the end of Part Three, there are several pages of problems to use in counselling role plays. The age-groups I have given relating to invented problems are suggested as loose guidelines. It is for the leader to judge the most appropriate problems for the group as a whole. It is also for the leader to judge whether students should be placed in one large group or divided into smaller groups, depending on how much guidance and support they will require.

Please note: The symbol ✔ denotes those pages which are photocopiable and may be reproduced for group work.

Remember to read through each session well in advance to ensure that it is suitable for everyone in the group.

Part I

Introduction

This section explores relationships between people and why some friendships fail with an aim to changing negative views of relationship behaviour into positive ones.

It is useful to understand our present social behaviour and how it has come about in order to change our future social behaviour. Once we are aware of the messages we have received from our environment we are better able to consider their validity and whether or not they give us a positive approach to interacting with others around us. Hindering thoughts can be re-programmed to free us from the bonds imposed upon us by negative experiences and unrewarding relationships.

Part One provides the first step to social skills training which can improve all aspects of life for people at all levels of social competence. The ability to form rewarding relationships has implications for interaction at home, work and leisure.

What are Friends?

Conchita

Joining her friends in the common room before class, Conchita made her face look sad and disappointed. Immediately, Rachel and Mandy went up to her and said, 'You didn't get it, did you?' Rachel put her arm around Conchita and said, 'I'm really sorry. If anyone deserved it, you did.'

Conchita could no longer hide her smile. Then she laughed with joy.

'You really got us going there!' Mandy said with a sigh of relief mingled with envy. She wished she could be talented like Conchita.

Conchita hugged them both. 'I'm so happy. Art school! It's all I wanted. Let's celebrate tonight.'

Task I (in one large or several smaller groups)

Think about Conchita's friends and your own and talk about:

(1) What are friends?

(2) What are friends for?

(3) What qualities do you think a friend should have? (Honesty? Loyalty?)

(4) What qualities do you give in friendship?

(5) Is it important to have things in common with friends? (For example, both of you liking the same music.) Why?

(6) What do you have in common with your friends?

Josh

Josh arrived just before class, walking past Conchita and her friends who were huddled in a group. Those three were never far away from each other. 'Discussing boyfriends, make-up and diets, no doubt,' Josh thought.

When he walked into his first session, Josh saw Nick and Dave sitting on the desks. 'All right?' Josh said as he threw his bag on the floor beside them, not bothering to watch as it slid into place beneath the desks.

'Done the essay?' Nick asked. He'd tried but had given up.

'Of sorts. The football was more interesting,' Josh replied. He'd had a hell of a weekend with his parents rowing and then turning on him. He hadn't been able to concentrate. The rows always upset him. 'Who's for a knockabout at lunch time?' Dave asked, kicking his foot in the air. Nick and Josh said, 'Yeah, OK.' It was better than sitting around.

Task 2 (in one large or several smaller groups)

Think about Josh's friends, Conchita's friends and your friends and talk about:

    (1)   What do girl friends often talk about?

    (2)   What do boy friends often talk about?

    (3)   What do many girl friends do when they are together?

    (4)   What do boy friends generally do when they are together?

    (5)   Is there a difference in closeness between Conchita's friendship group and Josh's friendship group? If so, how is it different?

Task 3 (in one large or several smaller groups)

Talk about:

(1) How close (intimate) are your friends to you? (Do you talk about personal things and give each other support or do you only talk about practical things like homework?)

(2) What makes some friends close and others less close? (We talk about different things to different friends. Some friends we tell our problems to, others we don't. Why is there this difference?)

(3) Often girl friendships are closer than boy friendships. Why is this? (Think about what qualities girls value and what qualities boys value, e.g. sympathy, leadership.) Are there other reasons why girls and boys behave differently in relationships? (For example, from whom do we learn and copy?)

Task 4 (in one large or several smaller groups)

Talk about: What sort of (social) support do we get from friends? In other words, what do we get out of these relationships? (Think of other people's friends as well as your own.)

What are Friends?

Task 1

(1) *What are friends?* A friend is someone with whom we share affection and regard (usually outside sexual and family bonds). A friend is someone we like (or love) and respect and they us. A friend is someone we enjoy being with.

(2) *What are friends for?* For support, for doing things together (such as sport) and for companionship. For sharing good and bad news. For celebrating and commiserating. (Conchita's friends were ready to give their support when they thought Conchita had bad news and when they knew it was good news.) For putting your friend's feelings before your own sometimes. (Like Mandy did – even though she was envious, she was happy for Conchita.) For recognising when someone needs help. For warmth and comfort. (Conchita's friends were physically close – they hugged.) For joking and teasing. (At first Conchita pretended she had bad news.)

(3) *What qualities do you think a friend should have?* Loyalty and faithfulness; reliability; sympathy; trustworthiness; helpfulness; understanding; honesty; intimacy.

(5) *Is it important to have things in common with friends? Why?* Yes. To have a sense of belonging. To share experiences. To talk about things that won't bore the other person. Relationships in adolescents are generally built on having similar social power, interests, abilities and life experiences. These similarities help to form a close-knit social network offering much support and understanding.

Tasks 2–4 of this session contain information from pages 74–77 of *The Anatomy of Relationships* by Michael Argyle and Monika Henderson (1985) published by Random House, and used with the permission of Peters Fraser and Dunlop, Writers' Agents.

Task 2

(1) *What do girl friends often talk about?* They are more likely to exchange confidences, discuss personal problems, relationships, their feelings about things that have happened, their feelings about other people, their boyfriends, clothes, fashion, make-up, body-size, diets, pop/film stars.

(2) *What do boy friends generally talk about?* They are more likely to talk about sport, what they've done, hobbies and films.

(3) *What do most girl friends do when they are together?* Much of their time is spent talking. They might go shopping together, go to each other's houses, see a film.

(4) *What do many boy friends do when they are together?* Male friendships are more likely to be based on action – boys get together to do things such as play or watch sport or take part in other leisure activities.

(5) *What is the difference in closeness between Conchita's friendship group and Josh's friendship group?* Conchita shows her feelings and shares the good and the bad times with her friends. Josh does not have any intimacy with his friends. He does not tell them what goes on at home. Boys may not discuss personal problems or emotional issues as much as girls.

Task 3

(2) *What makes some friends close and others less close?* It depends on how people respond to what we say and how we behave – and whether they seem genuinely interested in us or spend all their time talking about themselves. Others may not be able to keep confidences.

(3) *Girl friendships may be closer than boy friendships. Why is this?* Girls may value different qualities: warmth, sympathy, kindness, gentleness, cheerfulness. The qualities valued by boys may be: assertion, leadership, independence, self-reliance. People use their parents as role models. If a father doesn't have close friends or show qualities often attributed to women, their sons are not likely to either. Men may spend more time competing at sports and at work which develops skills that are contrary to cooperation and support. Boys may fear homosexuality. They may want the macho image of being a strong, independent man who needs no emotional support and hides weaknesses such as depression and stress.

Task 4

What sort of (social) support do we get from friends? In other words, what do we get out of these relationships?

- o Intimacy – a close and caring relationship that develops trust and a feeling of understanding (empathy) between the friends.
- o Confidant – we can tell a friend our problems and expect a sympathetic ear.
- o Confidence – friends encourage us and tell us when we are doing the right thing which increases our feeling of self-worth (self-esteem). It helps us cope with difficult things.

○ Practical help – help in everyday activities: help with homework or choosing the right clothes for an interview.

○ Informational help – finding things out for us, telling us things we need to know.

○ Being part of a social group (social integration) – being accepted by a group of friends and taking part in social activities such as outings, dancing, pubbing, clubbing, swimming, squash, and so on.

Influences on Relationships

From birth many things have influenced how we behave in our relationships. We need to think about what (and who) has influenced our relationship behaviour and decide whether these relationship messages are positive (helpful) or negative (unhelpful).

You learn from those around you

- *How to show feelings...* such as anger, love, liking, gratitude, pleasure, disappointment, anger, being upset.
- *How to look...* when you meet someone, when you say goodbye, when you are pleased, when you are angry, when you love.
- *How to solve arguments...* either by each of you giving way a little (compromise), or by aggression or by sulking.
- *How to treat...* people you love, strangers, friends, those whom you dislike, those who irritate you, family, teachers, bosses, neighbours, other people in authority.
- *How to get on...* with members of your family, friends, neighbours, classmates, teachers and other people in authority.
- *How to...* say thank you, no thank you, refuse a request, let someone down, say sorry.
- *What to do when you meet...* a stranger, a friend, a member of the family, a neighbour, someone in authority.
- *How to behave...* at parties, at church, at college, at work, at home, at a friend's house.
- *Behaviour to expect from...* parents, family, friends, neighbours, teachers, bosses, other people in authority.
- *What you deserve from...* parents, family, friends, neighbours, teachers, bosses, other people in authority.
- *What you are worth to...* your parents, other members of your family, friends, neighbours, teachers, bosses, other people in authority.

- *What things are most important to…* parents, friends, family, neighbours, teachers, bosses and so on.
- *How to value…* relationships with different people such as friends, family or neighbours and what different people do for you.

Sally

Sally was often lonely and bored at home. She was an only child and her parents rarely invited other friends for her to play with. Her parents were very strict and Sally often got hit for not doing as she was told even when she really didn't deserve it. Her parents did not accept any back-chat and often Sally felt it was safer not to speak at all rather than risk her parents' anger.

Not many visitors came to the house as Sally's parents had few friends and those they did have always rang to arrange a meeting rather than turn up on the doorstep. Sally's grandparents also kept themselves very much to themselves and were not that interested in Sally. If she hung around them and they were busy they would buy her off with sweets to keep her happy.

Task 1 (in one large or several smaller groups)

(1) *What relationship messages does Sally get from her family?*
Example: Sally must learn to amuse herself without relying on other people.

(2) *Are these messages positive or negative? Why?*
Example: Negative. Sally will feel she is not worth her family spending time with her or making an effort to keep her happy.

(3) *How are these messages likely to affect Sally?*
Example: She will feel bad about herself (have a low self-esteem).

Task 2 (in one large or several smaller groups)

(1) *What relationship messages do you get from members of your family?* (Parents, grandparents, brothers, sisters, aunts and uncles.)

Are these positive or negative?

Example 1: My parents always shouted and threw things when they argued.

 Message: Solve arguments by fighting.
 Negative: This doesn't get you anywhere except make you more angry and upset.

Example 2: My parents always sat down together when they had a problem and tried to find a solution.

 Message: Cooperation gets results.
 Positive: Neither person feels bad and things aren't said in a temper that might later be regretted.

(2) *What relationship messages do you get from other sources?* (Films, famous people, advertising, people in the community.) Are they positive or negative (good ideas or bad ideas on how you should behave in a relationship)?

Give examples.

Influences on Relationships

Task 1

(1) *What relationship messages does Sally get from her family?*

- Obedience is more important than understanding how Sally feels or knowing why she does certain things.

- Sally's emotional needs are unimportant and are ignored.

- She is seen as a nuisance (when her grandparents give her sweets to keep her quiet and out of the way). She is not worthy of their valuable time and attention.

- Relationships are for convenience rather than for fun, for support or for showing affection and concern.

(2) *Are these messages positive or negative? Why?*

- The messages are negative. Sally is not learning to find her own way through the social maze with all its rules and rewards. She is being overshadowed by the negative sides of relationships. Her parent's relationships are functional – they arrange to meet a friend, catch up on the latest news and then do not see one another until another mutually convenient time. Most friendships do not work like this.

(3) *How are these messages likely to affect Sally?*

- Sally is being deprived of all the positive sides of relationships. She gets no affection from her parents or grandparents and they do not recognise her emotional needs by inviting friends round for her. She will approach people in a timid and apologetic way when making friends as though they are doing her a favour by talking to her – instead she should approach them as an equal, without expecting every encounter to end in failure or, at best, a superficial, non-intimate relationship.

- Spontaneous (spur of the moment) socialisation is likely to unsteady her as she sees her parents have to plan any meetings with the few friends they have.

- Her social expectations will not be high. As her parents have so few friends, Sally will not expect to have many and she will not expect to find them very rewarding. (She won't expect to enjoy their company very much.)

○ Sally will be timid in social situations and unable to relax – Sally prefers to stay quiet at home and is likely to be very careful about conversations with her own friends, worrying about saying the wrong thing and being disliked for it.

Task 2 of this session is based on information obtained from pages 23–24 of *Human Relationship Skills* by Professor Richard Nelson-Jones (1990) reproduced with the permission of Cassell plc, Wellington House, 125 Strand, London, England.

Task 2

(1) *What relationship messages do you get from members of your family?*

○ *Parents/guardians:* Parents who argue and shout at each other a great deal do not show how to deal with conflict without aggression or how to resolve differences of opinion through compromise (thus giving a negative experience). But loving and mutually supportive parents teach caring and negotiating skills (a positive experience).

○ *Brothers and sisters:* If parents treat you differently to your brothers and sisters, they may become jealous of you or you of them. It emphasises the difference between them and you, making them feel more or less important or trustworthy. For example, it may be a negative experience for your twin brother to be given more freedom because he is a boy and you are a girl (although under certain conditions this may be understandable since girls tend to be more vulnerable to attack at night).

If your parents encourage closeness between siblings by including everyone in family outings and stressing the importance of support, showing through their actions how to be friendly with one another, you acquire a good grounding for any relationship and will be encouraged to maintain support between your siblings into adult life (a positive experience).

○ *Grandparents:* If they listen to you, spend much time with you and are affectionate, they give you positive messages about relationships. If they see you as a nuisance when you are a child they are not treating you with respect or acknowledging that you are a person with feelings (negative messages). Sometimes grandparents are the main carers in which case their influence will be greater.

○ *Aunts and uncles:* Regular contact can build up a rapport with a generation similar to that of your parents and can give alternative messages on how to behave or they can strengthen existing positive ones (positive experience). However, if they reinforce your parents views and values which you strongly disagree with, then you may consider this a negative experience, having no alternative input to family life.

○ *Older friends:* You can see the effects of their behaviour in their own lives and have immediate feedback on whether their approach to socialising is worthwhile or harmful for developing good relationships.

(2) *What relationship messages do you get from other sources?*

○ *Community leaders:* For example, priests, doctors, sports coaches, leaders of clubs, such as scouts or guides. All of these can give different impressions of behaviour in different settings. For example, a doctor or priest may give a formal impression (they may be expected to act professionally with their 'clients' and are more likely to give negative messages to those who do not hold the same views). Leaders of clubs and sports coaches, on the other hand, may give an informal impression. Their task to develop other aspects of your character may involve a familiar coaxing approach (they are more likely to give positive messages since there are common points of agreement through voluntarily attending such clubs).

○ *Peer groups:* Friends at school/college. It is easy to see the differences in bullying (negative) and supportive (positive) behaviour. The way you choose to behave with your peers depends on your personal experiences – whether to join in with aggressive friends, or to reject them and concentrate on relationships that do not centre around putting other people down. How you have been treated by your peers also determines your future behaviour towards others.

○ *Teachers:* Teachers can be very strong role models. If a teacher singles out students for ridicule, deliberately making them feel small in front of their peers, they are giving a negative message of not caring for the other person's feelings – a message that their own satisfaction is paramount.

However, a teacher who asks students to stay behind at the end of the lesson to discuss an embarrassing matter shows respect and a positive awareness of their feelings. A teacher may also be able to discern the difference between a student who can take an abrasive comment in class and a more timid student, who has offended for the first time and would not respond well to a public reprimand. This is a truer picture of how people behave – we relate to different people in a different way depending on how they behave towards us.

○ *Famous people:* Bob Geldof and other people frequently mentioned by the media for their good deeds may influence people's aspirations and give them a direction in life – what to aim for and how to do it – in Bob Geldof's case through music (the Live Aid Rock Concert in 1985 and its spin-offs).

Some people could be either a positive role model or a negative one, depending on what your values are: for example, the Pope or politicians. Roman Catholics may support the Pope's view on family planning, but others may feel that this view contributes to poverty and over-population in some countries. A politician may have a social policy that pleases one portion of the population while the same policy affronts another group – such as the single parents who have had their benefit reduced. Within different contexts both the Pope and politicians may perceive their roles as of benefit to society. It is up to the individual to decide whether their approaches are to be respected and emulated. Paul Gascoigne who was reported to be guilty of domestic violence was still revered because of his outstanding ability to play football.

o *Fictional people:* Copying the antics of *Just William* or *My Naughty Little Sister*, instead of merely delighting in the fictional exploration of naughtiness, would not give you a positive experience since you have to face the unpleasant consequences of any wrong-doings.

   Superman fights against evil and helps those in trouble – there are predominantly positive qualities to this character.

o *Advertising:* People behaving in specific ways with the purpose of influencing purchasing decisions.

   o Negative example – in a car advert, one partner leaves the other after a row and is only interested in taking possession of the car. The message here is not to stay and sort out your difficulties, it is telling you to get out with what is most important in your life – a material item.

   o Positive example – in a tissue advert, friends are sitting together, sympathising with one who has a cold while one of them solicitously hands over another tissue showing care and concern.

Personal Development

Personal development is forming your character to cope with life in a way which suits you best. It is getting to know and understand the real you. It helps you achieve the life goals that you, personally, have set.

Personal development helps you make the most of yourself. It is also individual (people have different ideas on what they want and how to get it).

Personal development may be held back by bad experiences. It is our choice whether we ignore any social problems we might have (the easier but lonelier choice) or to work at developing our people-skills to greatly improve our relationships.

Georgio

Georgio was often ill when he was young and even now, in his teens, he picks up more colds and 'flu than his friends. Georgio is not often allowed out on his own and never in the evenings unless he is collected by a responsible adult. His parents are very worried about his safety even though Georgio does not live in a particularly dangerous area and he is never out after eleven.

Georgio has never been allowed to stay overnight at a friend's house or go on school trips, except for day-trips. He is jealous his friends have much more freedom. His parents have to approve of any friend Georgio brings home and they are very particular about his friends' backgrounds. His parents are rather snobbish.

Task I (in one large or several smaller groups)

(1) *What negative messages has Georgio received from his upbringing?*

Example: If Georgio does not do as his parents say he will suffer for It, through illness or from being attacked or mugged at night.

(2) *How do you think Georgio's personal development will be affected by these messages?*

Example: Georgio may feel very worried or guilty if he does something his parents disapprove of since they over-react.

Colin

At home Colin was naughty just to get attention. Then he would get hit with Dad's belt (unless Dad was too busy hitting Mum to notice what Colin had done). At school he found the work hard so he clowned around – no one took him seriously and Colin didn't have any close friends. He didn't fit in and he hated being the class dunce. Nobody ever expected his name to be mentioned unless it was for something bad. He felt that school had failed him – so he didn't owe anyone there any favours. There was a group of lads from a different class that hung around together in a gang and Colin joined them. He wanted to feel he belonged somewhere. But to get into this gang, he had to fall in line with the rest of them. And that meant shoplifting, stealing from the cloakrooms and bullying the weeds.

Task 2 (in one large or several smaller groups)

(1) *What negative messages has Colin received from his upbringing?*

Example: His parents don't love him.

(2) *How do you think Colin's personal development will be affected by these messages?*

Example: He will feel bad about himself (low self-esteem) and be angry at others because of it (aggressive).

Socially unacceptable behaviour is highest when groups of friends are formed into gangs that aim for negative rather than positive interests.

Task 3 (in small groups)

(1) *What are the effects of having negative relationships on your personal development?*

Example: I enjoy frightening people – it makes me feel powerful.

(2) *What are the effects of having positive relationships on your personal development?*

Example: The support of close friends that care about me makes me feel secure.

Task 4 (in one large or several smaller groups)

Bullying includes unkind teasing, spread of malicious gossip, taunting and baiting as well as physical attacks, extortion and sexual harassment.

Talk about:

- Why do people bully?
- What affect does bullying have on the victim?
- What should we do about bullies?

Personal Development

Task 1

(1) *What negative messages has Georgio received from his upbringing?*

- o If Georgio does not do as his parents say he will suffer for it – through illness or from being attacked or mugged at night.
- o Georgio has to be very careful with the friends he chooses – it's not just a matter of whom he likes and gets on well with, their background is also important.
- o If Georgio has any friends his parents might not approve of, he probably has to be careful not to talk about them – he has to be secretive.
- o Not letting Georgio stay overnight at a friend's house suggests his parents don't trust him and that he is not safe in anyone else's care.
- o School trips and joining in the fun are not as important as keeping well and safe, even when there is no real danger.
- o Just because his friends are allowed to do things it doesn't mean that Georgio can.

(2) *How do you think Georgio's personal development will be affected by these messages?*

- o He may have difficulty becoming an independent adult as he is used to having decisions made for him (he is over-protected). Georgio is unlikely to be adventurous or to take reasonable risks (unless he rebels and goes to the other extreme of being reckless).
- o Georgio may develop too strong a conscience with feelings of anxiety and guilt if he feels he might be doing something of which his parents disapprove.
- o Fearing disapproval may hamper his desire to make new friends, leaving him dependent on his parents for social contact.
- o Georgio's lack of independence has not given him the necessary experience to make his own decisions and learn to stand up for himself.
- o Georgio's personality has largely been directed by his parents as he is always overshadowed by them.

Task 2

(1)   *What negative messages has Colin received from his upbringing?*

- o   To get any attention, Colin has to behave badly. He knows his parents don't love him.

- o   Colin is a failure in school and socially. He knows this because his parents don't show him any affection and his class mates don't want him as a friend.

- o   The only way to be accepted into a group or gang is to unquestioningly do what is expected of him. He is being led rather than leading or acting independently.

- o   No one in Colin's family expresses their feelings verbally so Colin won't see talking things over as a valuable experience, he is more likely to bottle feelings inside him.

(2)   *How do you think Colin's personal development will be affected by these messages?*

- o   Colin feels parentally rejected which makes him angry as his parents should be the ones who care most for him.

- o   He is more likely to be delinquent and aggressive because of the pent up anger inside him. There is no other way he knows of getting rid of his bad feelings about himself.

- o   Colin is less likely to develop friendly, socially skilled behaviour, a conscience, concern for others, cooperative behaviour or a sense of belonging – at home, school/college or at work. Colin is unable to form intimate relationships which limits the rewards he can acquire.

- o   Colin has not been shown any caring or loving skills and so is not likely to display them. He is not used to expressing his feelings, so bottles them up inside.

- o   If Colin's negative relationships continue then he is likely to become even more deviant. Colin's own identity is overshadowed by group or gang identity. In extreme cases of negative influence, he could commit serious offences.

- o   A lack of responsibility and poor communication works against a mutual sharing of problems.

- o   Colin's experience of home life may contribute towards frequent rows and break-ups when he has a partner and may be responsible for the repetition of domestic violence witnessed. Then his children may well continue the cycle.

Task 3

(1)   *What are the effects of having negative relationships on your personal development?* See above for ideas.

(2)   *What are the effects of having positive relationships on your personal development?*

- o Skilful parenting allows children to develop into emotionally independent adults.
- o A secure child will have the confidence in adolescence to seek independence of his parents and will have developed high self-esteem, high self-confidence, a desire for independence, a sense of identity, assertiveness, securing a place within a social structure (belonging to a network or having many friends) and social activity (people to do things with and go places with).

Task 4

(1) *Why do people bully?*

- o Bullies enjoy hurting others and making them feel uncomfortable and frightened.
- o People bully to demand respect, and, if they are in a group, to give the group social identity or importance.
- o Bullying expresses a desire for power, dominance and control over others through negative means.
- o Many people who bully in a group would not do so if they were on their own.

(2) *What effect does bullying have on the victim?*

- o Victims tend to be timid, unassertive, shy, afraid, lacking in confidence and often perceived as different in some way, for example, have no friends, have a stammer, or are of a different race.
- o The victim may find it hard to trust people and feel confident about himself.
- o Bullying gives people poor self-esteem and may put them in a 'victim' frame of mind so that throughout their lives they are targeted as vulnerable people and taken advantage of.
- o Some victims commit suicide.

(3) *What should we do about bullies?*

- o If young bullies are not helped to deal with their aggression (anger) they will continue to bully and be aggressive throughout life. They may need counselling to come to terms with why they need to bully (perhaps they were abused at home) and to break the cycle, so that their children are not brought up in an aggressive manner and become bullies themselves.
- o We need to tell someone in a position of authority or power about what is happening. (At work, it may be your boss's boss you tell about being sexually harassed.)

Social Networks

Friendships are part of a large picture of social contacts known as the social network.

Amita

Amita's parents control whom she sees outside school. They belong to a close Asian community. Ideally they would like her to mix only with other Asian girls, so that she does not want things her parents do not approve of, like having a boyfriend or going out unaccompanied by her mother or aunt, or even wanting to go to parties with friends from school. The only contact Amita is allowed to have outside school (with her own age group) is with children of her parents' friends — when families get together for different celebrations. At other times Amita is at home with her family. She is not allowed to accept any invitations from friends at school.

Task 1 (in one large or several smaller groups)

Amita is only allowed to mix with people of her own race.

(1) What are the positive points to this rule?

(2) What are the negative points to this rule?

Please note, it is inappropriate to make value-judgements. This example is merely used to illustrate a scenario where freedom is limited. It is this restricted freedom in relation to social skills and personal development that is under discussion, not the pros and cons of Asian family life and culture.

Joe

Joe is a member of a young Christian fellowship group that meets weekly. The group has bible readings, says prayers, sings songs, arranges outings about once a month, often has guest speakers and has services on Sundays. Joe enjoys these prayer meetings and is glad of the friendship that belonging to the fellowship gives him, but he is very aware that friendships with others are not considered good by the group as they will lead him away from Christianity. Joe later meets Charlotte, who is an atheist. Joe starts to go out with her. When he tells the group members about her, they say he must finish with her as she will lead him away from God.

Task 2 (in one large or several smaller groups)

(1)   What does the fellowship have to offer Joe?

(2)   How would you describe the friendships Joe has there?

(3)   What might happen if Joe did something the fellowship did not approve of?

Task 3 (in one large or several smaller groups)

Amita and Joe belong to cliques.

(1)   What is a clique?

(2)   What sort of cliques are there?

(3)   What makes cliques different from other social groups?

Carrie

Carrie's mum has cancer and has been given one year to live. Carrie finds it impossible to imagine what life will be like without Mum and feels she's cracking up. Her school work is suffering and she has become very irritable with everyone. Her close friends have not been in her situation and do not know what to do to help. They talk to their parents about her who talk to people they know. They pass to Carrie 'phone numbers of a recommended counsellor and a self-help group to help families in similar situations.

John

John joins a local alcoholic's group. He can only discuss his problem with others in the same situation and has come to rely on their support. John's Dad comes home after being missing for three years. John finds this new situation hard to cope with. He no longer knows his Dad and he'd convinced himself his Dad was dead. Too much has changed. John goes to the off licence to buy whiskey. But before he opens the bottle, he calls someone from the group. His friend tells him to stay put and not do anything. He'll be there in five minutes.

Task 4 (in groups)

Carrie belongs to a loose social network. John belongs to a clique.
  (1)   When are loose social networks better than cliques?
  (2)   When are cliques better than loose social networks?

In Figure 4.1, I am the central bubble 'Me'. My friends are represented by letters and numbers. Friends 1 to 12 are from my childhood, attending university and working at my first job. (They were single and childless, like me.) Friends A to H were made after I'd married and had moved to a completely different area. (They are all married and have children, like me.) 1 to 9 and A and B are friends who do not meet up with any others in my network. 10, 11, 12 form a small clique. (We all worked in the same school.) C to H socialise (meet up) with each other as well as with me. We form a clique. (We all live within close walking distance and we all have young children.)

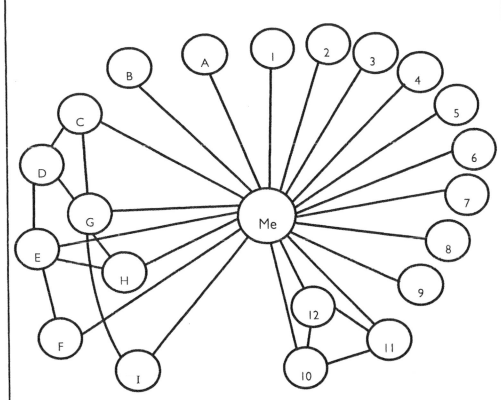

Figure 4.1 Social Network Diagram

Task 5 (on your own)

(1)   List the people in your social network. Then draw a diagram to show the patterns of interaction (who socialises with whom).

(2)   Is this network a clique, a loose network or a mixture of the two?

If you prefer you may draw a social network for someone else such as a friend or relative. Then say what type it is.

Social Networks

Task 1

(1) *What are the positive points to this rule?*

- o Amita is protected from outside influences so that she can fulfil her expected cultural and religious role and keep her standing within this close community.
- o Amita need not worry over making decisions as these are made for her.
- o Amita will be more likely to make a good marriage as her virtues are assured.
- o Amita can be sure of parental and community support throughout her life.

(2) *What are the negative points to this rule?*

- o Amita's personality is not allowed to develop in a way she chooses.
- o Amita has had little personal learning experience which is valuable. Amita lacks self-discovery as a whole range of social experiences and how she reacts to them are denied her.
- o Amita is likely to bring her own children up in exactly the same way since she has nothing else to compare her upbringing with.
- o Restricted social experience reduces Amita's understanding of people.
- o Amita may be timid and feel insecure since she was not allowed to develop independence and may be unsure how to behave in many social situations.

Task 2

(1) *What does the fellowship have to offer Joe?*

- o It offers Joe friendship within a close, secure and caring community.
- o It provides a variety of activities and develops Joe's spirituality.
- o It instils high moral values – although this may make Joe more critical of others and more exacting in his personal requirements for any relationships.

(2) *How would you describe the friendships Joe has there?*

- o They are judgemental and conditional on Joe conforming.
- o It may be that new members are persuaded to join the group merely because of the companionship on offer. And this may not be genuine.

> o These friends may be ideal in understanding Joe's emotional and spiritual
> needs and may provide a ready listener for things Joe cannot discuss with
> anyone else.

(3) *What might happen if Joe did something the fellowship did not approve of?*

> o The members may withdraw their friendship. He may be shunned and
> labelled as a non-Christian which would make him feel bad about himself.

Tasks 3 and 4 of this session contain information obtained from page 69 of *The Anatomy of Relationships* by Michael Argyle and Monika Henderson (1985) published by Random House, and reproduced with the permission of Peters Fraser and Dunlop, Writers' Agents.

Task 3

(1) *What is a clique?*

> o A clique is a small, exclusive (not everyone can join) group of people who are
> mutually friendly. A clique is a dense social network.

(2) *What sort of cliques are there?*

> o Usually clique members have something in common – such as the same
> culture and/or religion, or belong to the same club or because they all have
> the same jobs (a group of teachers or doctors or solicitors). A clique may be
> political (such as the Members of Parliament) or might link people secretly as
> in the Freemasons.

(3) *What makes cliques different from other social groups?*

> o Members of a social clique tend not to make new friends, having all the social
> support they need. Its members keep the network as it is, without any
> breaking away through mutual support and frequency of meetings. They are
> expected to conform to any rules because of fear of rejection from the
> network. A clique can be professional as well as social and would then have
> very specific rules of behaviour, such as for Members of Parliament.
> Members of a clique tend to be very similar, for example, racially, politically,
> religiously, by class or social standing.

Task 4

(1) *When are loose social networks better than cliques?*

> o The members of a loose network have a greater variety of interests and
> backgrounds. (Members will not necessarily be of the same class, religion,
> race, age, sex or background.) Loose networks are better at providing
> informational help as each member has friends outside the network and they,
> in turn, have other contacts – the group knowledge is not as limited. Word

takes longer to get round but there is a greater range of skills. Looser groups are more open to new additions or changes or linking up with another social network than with cliques. There are more opportunities for mixing with and meeting new people. Loose networks are less intense and demanding on its members. With a clique, if you do something the group strongly disapproves of you might lose all your friends in one go.

(2)   *When are cliques better than loose social networks?*

o In times of crisis the support of a clique is much stronger as each member is closely involved with all the other members. They are less likely to separate into smaller networks or lose a member.

Making New Friends

The development of a friendship can be divided into three steps. Talk about what happens at each step in one large group.

Step 1: The first meeting

Gareth sits opposite a girl (Zoe) on the train. He thinks she looks pretty. He doesn't have a girlfriend and wants to get to know her better.

(1)   What must Gareth do to get to know the girl?

(2)   What could go wrong?

Step 2: The next meeting

Gareth and Zoe are spending the evening in a pub. Later, Gareth will walk her home and Zoe will invite him in for coffee (having asked her parents first).

(3)   What does Gareth need to do to make a good impression?

(4)   What does Zoe need to do to make a good impression?

(5)   What could go wrong?

Step 3: Becoming intimate

Gareth and Zoe get on well and like each other.

Zoe

Zoe hasn't been quite honest with Gareth. She has been hiding something from him. Before they get any more involved, Zoe feels she has to tell him, even though she's worried about what he'll do.

(6)   What might Zoe have to tell Gareth?

(7)   What might Gareth do? How might this secret affect him?

Gareth

Gareth survived Zoe's secret and wants her to sleep with him. His friends have been asking how far they've gone and he feels he needs to keep up with his best mate who has sex with his girlfriend.

(8) Why might Zoe say no to sleeping with Gareth? Does this make their friendship less worthwhile?

(9) Why might Zoe say yes to sleeping with Gareth?

A couple of weeks later, Zoe bumps into three of Gareth's friends in the street.

(10) What might go wrong between Zoe and Gareth because of this meeting?

The example just used is merely an illustration. When you make a new friend, these three steps are the same whether the friend is to become a partner or a close friend of either sex. The problems at each stage are also similar – for example, whether you can make conversation, make a good impression, not upset the other person beyond repair, and so on. A filtering out of friendship can occur at any of these stages, stopping the friendship from developing further.

Task 1 (in small groups)

Think of a friendship that did not develop well.

(1) How did it start?

(2) How did it develop (if at all)?

(3) When did things start to go wrong? (Or when did you know that this friendship would not develop?)

(4) How did you know these things? What gave you the messages?

Most people agree on what behaviour is desired or expected in a friendship. (This could be described as a form of 'friendship code'.) If you do not stick to this, you may have difficulty in making and keeping friends.

Task 2 (in groups)

(1) What do you think a 'friendship code' could include?

(2) What do you think are the most important reasons for friendship break-ups? Place these in order of importance.

Task 3 (in groups)

How can you widen your social circle? (What can you do to make it possible to meet new friends?)

Making New Friends

The ideas in this session are loosely adapted from pages 70–74 of *The Anatomy of Relationships* by Michael Argyle and Monika Henderson (1985) published by Random House, and used with the permission of Peters Fraser and Dunlop, Writers' Agents.

Step 1: The first meeting

(1) *What can Gareth do to get to know this person?*

Smile, say hello, make some comment about the weather, about how crowded the train is, that he hadn't seen her before on this route, that it was his first time on this route, that he was going to be late, that he was nervous about his first day at work. He can tell her his name and ask her what she is called if she doesn't volunteer it. If he wants to see her again he should say so – or he can ask whether she is always on that train to make sure he catches it in future (so he may bump into her another time).

(2) *What could go wrong?*
- She might not like the look of him.
- She might not like being 'chatted up'.
- She might not live in the area – the journey she's making could be a one-off.
- She might not think much about what he has to say.
- She might be too nervous about talking to strangers.
- She might already have a boyfriend.
- Gareth may not have good social skills, or she may be too shy to respond.

Step 2: The next meeting

(3) *What should Gareth do to make a good impression?*
- He should arrive on time, smile and look pleased to see Zoe.
- He can dress in something nice.
- He must listen to what she has to say and show interest in her views.
- He must anticipate her needs and be considerate.
- He needs to balance what she tells him with information about himself.

(4) *What does Zoe need to do to make a good impression?*

    ○ All of the above.

(5) *What could go wrong?*

They could say something to put the other off – like telling a secret too early. They could learn that they have nothing in common with the other person or that they are very different in some way. (Different religious or political beliefs, upbringing, wealth, sexuality.) One of them could get drunk, swear too much, make rude jokes, offer drugs, be loud and embarrassing. Not being able to think of anything to talk about. Not being rewarding enough – not smiling or looking at the other person, or being boring by talking about themselves all the time. Not being kind and considerate.

Step 3: Becoming intimate

(6) *What might Zoe have to tell Gareth?*

    ○ She'd had an abortion.

    ○ She was a virgin.

    ○ She wasn't a virgin.

    ○ She'd been raped or sexually abused.

    ○ She was on drugs.

    ○ She was a lesbian or bisexual.

(7) *What might Gareth do? How might this secret affect him?*

If he was very religious, Gareth may reject her if she's had an abortion or slept with someone. If she was raped Gareth might not know how to handle it or be understanding about the trauma she's suffering – he may not show patience or understanding of the physical side of their relationship. Gareth may not want a lesbian or bisexual friend – even for companionship, so the relationship would end here.

Gareth

(8) *Why might Zoe say no to sleeping with Gareth? Does this make their friendship less worthwhile?*

    ○ Zoe might not want to feel pressured into sleeping with Gareth.

    ○ Zoe may want more time to get to know him better.

    ○ It might be against Zoe's religious or moral principles.

    ○ Zoe may feel that Gareth does not love her but only lusts after her.

(9) *Why might Zoe say yes to sleeping with Gareth?*

- She wants to become closer to him.
- She is in love and sees it as a natural progression of their affection for each other.

(10) *What might go wrong between Zoe and Gareth because of this meeting?*

Gareth's friends may make it obvious that Gareth has told them Zoe is sleeping with him. Gareth's friends may let Zoe know that they know her secret. Both of the above examples are to do with confidentiality – breaking confidentiality could be the end of the relationship.

Task 2

Taken from Tables 6 and 7, pages 92 and 93 from *The Anatomy of Relationships* (see page 42).

The ten most important factors in the break-up of friendships (the most important factor listed first):

- Being jealous or critical of the person's other relationships.
- Discussing with others what had been told in confidence.
- Not volunteering help in time of need.
- Not trusting or confiding.
- Criticising the person in public.
- Not showing positive regard for the person.
- Not standing up for you in your absence.
- Not being tolerant of the person's other friends.
- Not showing emotional support.
- Nagging.

Friends also:

- Respect the other's privacy.
- Trust and confide in each other.
- Show emotional support.
- Look the other in the eye during conversation.
- Strive to make the other happy while in your company.
- Share news of success.
- Ask for personal advice.
- Joke or tease with the other person.
- Seek to repay debts, favours and compliments.
- Disclose personal problems and feelings to the other person.

Task 3

How can you widen your social circle?

- Join evening classes.
- Join a leisure centre or sports club.
- Join a regular group such as Ramblers.
- Accept invitations.
- Do voluntary work.
- Join an amateur dramatics society or a choir.
- Offer help when someone needs it.
- Help in a local church/community.
- Talk to people you meet.
- Be friendly to those around you.
- Invite people to your home.
- Go out more to give you more to talk about.
- Improve your confidence by going to assertiveness training classes (or similar).
- Improve your social skills.

SESSION 6

Loneliness

Many people are lonely. We need to feel part of a group or couple for a sense of belonging and to be seen to fit in. We also need friends to help us learn how to get on with people and for support that cannot be provided by the family.

Kwesi

Kwesi has lived most of his life in Ghana in Africa, but has recently moved to England. He finds the weather cold and miserable and the college unfriendly. People only speak to him to answer his questions. Most of the time he is ignored. Sometimes, a group of girls mimic his accent and if he has to talk to them they never understand him first time. They often giggle behind his back.

He is the only black student in the year and feels he doesn't belong. He's tried to join in and make friends but it hasn't worked. Once he went up to a group that were listening to a joke but no one started again for him or explained what it was about. He felt stupid.

Kwesi also hears jokes made about the sandwiches his mother makes him. They try to guess what he's eating. And when they talk about music, someone always brings up the subject of drums whenever he is within earshot.

Task I (in one large or several smaller groups)

Talk about:

(1) In what ways is Kwesi made to feel left out?

(2) How could the students at college make him feel welcome?

Wendy

Wendy's father is rich and their family live in a big house just out of town. Most of the girls at Wendy's school have never been there because Wendy rarely invites anyone. There's no one at school who's really good enough to be her friend so she imagines friends instead.

Polly

Polly goes to Wendy's school and has lots of friends. She was very happy until six months ago when her mother died. Since then, she's been very quiet and hardly ever smiles. She wants to talk to someone about what happened, but all her friends have both parents alive and wouldn't understand. She misses her mum dreadfully — and so does her Dad. He hardly talks either.

Task 2 (in one large or several smaller groups)

Wendy and Polly are both lonely.

(1) Why is Wendy lonely?

(2) Why is Polly lonely?

(3) How would you describe their different types of loneliness?

(4) *Are there other reasons for being lonely?*

Gary

Gary went to school alone, sat in class alone and came home from school alone. He'd become used to being ignored but didn't like it. If he ever thought he was being stared at, he'd turn round and shout, 'What're you looking at?' He'd also pull a really nasty face. He wasn't going to let anyone mess around with him.

One day, a boy laughed at Gary when he tripped up the step when going into class. Gary spun round and stamped on the other boy's foot. Now it was his turn to laugh. No one was going to get one over on him. Anyway, soon he'd be out of there. He was going to leave school the moment he turned sixteen.

Task 3 (in one large or several smaller groups)

Talk about:

   (1)   How does being unpopular affect Gary?

   (2)   What does it feel like to be left out?

Christine

Christine is 25 years old. She had few friends in school and even less now. But she's joined a dating agency. Her husband, when she's found him, will fill her lonely hours. She doesn't need anyone else.

Christine's studying hard to get a better job. She's already done well for herself but she has ambition to do better. And on weekends, Christine reads all those classics she meant to when she was younger and never had the time. And when she isn't reading she writes her diary. It's useful to write down her thoughts and feelings. Her diary is rather like a close friend — except it's better at keeping secrets.

Task 4 (in one large or several smaller groups)

Talk about:

   (1)   How has Christine tried to make up for a lack of friends?

   (2)   What are risks of being lonely?

Loneliness

Task 1

(1) *In what ways is Kwesi made to feel left out?*

- Private jokes – laughing behind his back.
- Not filling him in when he arrived half way through the joke.
- Being ignored.
- Having jokes made about his food and frequent reference to drums.

(2) *How could the students at college make him feel welcome?*

- Ask about his home and customs.
- Ask about the food he eats and to describe what it tastes like or ask to taste some.
- Ask him what music he likes – not assuming that because he is from Africa, he only knows and likes drums.
- Try to understand his accent without making it obvious.
- Explain any jokes he overhears or fill him in on any conversation he's missed if he arrives half-way through.

Task 2

(1) *Why is Wendy lonely?*

She is lonely, because she has no friends. Wendy has too high expectations of her friends and thinks that there is no one good enough for her. She is too proud.

(2) *Why is Polly lonely?*

She is lonely, because she has no one to share her feelings with. She feels no one could understand what she's going through, even though she has many friends.

(3) *How would you describe their different types of loneliness?*

Wendy's loneliness is social – she doesn't have friends to do things with or to be with. Social loneliness is when we feel bored, without an aim and on the outside or edge of things.

Polly's loneliness is emotional — it is her feelings that are not shared even though she has plenty of friends. Emotional loneliness is when we feel abandoned, empty, worried and frightened.

(4) *Are there other reasons for being lonely?*

- Being socially rejected and ignored.
- Experiencing divorce of parents or of being abandoned, if one parent leaves.
- By moving to a new area and having to make new friends, by changing jobs or by going away to college when other school friends stay at home and find work — the friends left behind form closer friendships with other, more available, people. The student, home in the holidays, then has the additional burden of having less in common with friends at home.

Task 3

(1) *How does being unpopular affect Gary?*

- Gary has become aggressive (angry in an uncontrolled way) and hostile (unfriendly) towards other people.
- He is probably leaving school early because he has no rewarding relationships there and doesn't feel part of the school.
- He is lonely.
- He lacks social skills. (Growling at people is not a positive way of communicating.)
- He behaves as though he dislikes other people. He doesn't look for nice things to say about them.
- He has a low opinion of himself — he expects to be made fun of.
- He is very much on his own — he probably lacks cooperative skills.
- Since he has had bad experiences, he probably doesn't trust people.

(2) *What does it feel like to be left out?*

Something wrong with me	Hatred towards others
Wary of meeting people	Frightened of life
Dread of social situations	Frightened of being alone
Self-conscious	On the outside looking in
Worthless	Depressed
A joke	Unloveable
Suicidal	An outcast
Not likeable	Angry
Isolated	Miserable
Bitter	Embarrassed

Task 4

(1) *How has Christine tried to make up for a lack of friends?*

- o She is trying to find a sexual partner to fill all the gaps of friendship instead of working at improving her relationships in general.
- o She is putting most of her time and energy into work to fill the gaps from not socialising.
- o She is filling her time with other non-social activities – reading, writing her diary.

(2) *What are risks of being lonely?*

- o Loneliness can lead to depression and even to suicide. People who feel that they have no one to turn to can be very vulnerable in times of crises. (Suicide is greatest in the 15 to 24 age group.)
- o There is nothing to balance conflict and lack of emotional reward if living within an unsupportive family.
- o Lonely people tend not to live as long and can be harder hit by illness.

Barriers in Friendships

If friends are not open and honest, the relationship may fail or not develop. Ideally, we want a deep understanding of one another so that we can become close.

> *Lack of openness*: "Yes, I'm fed up, but I don't want to talk about it."

The person with a lack of openness has admitted to there being something wrong but is not prepared to say why.

> *Lack of honesty*: "I'm fine, so just leave me alone."

The person with a lack of honesty denies that there is anything wrong at all and so completely shuts out the other person.

We choose whom we tell certain things and we are careful about whom to trust. We do not have to tell our best friend everything. Sometimes we need time to think things through before we want to discuss it with someone else. But if we regularly clam up, we put up too many barriers and won't have close friendships.

Task 1 (in one large or several smaller groups)

Talk about:

(1)   When and why have you been dishonest in a relationship?

(2)   If you know your friend is being dishonest, would you confront them or ignore the dishonesty?

Task 2 (in one large or several smaller groups)

Talk about:

(1) If you discover something about a classmate's family would you:

- Tease them about it?
- Tell everyone?
- Keep it quiet and wait to see if the person ever brings the subject up?
- Have a quiet word with the person to see if they want to talk about it?

(2) Which would most likely make you both friends? Why?

Task 3 (in one large or several smaller groups)

(1) Do you set up any other barriers? If so, what and why?

Example: rejection of any physical contact – quite common in males from a Western culture.

(2) If you reject physical comfort from a friend do you think they will ever offer it again? How would you feel if your touch had been rejected?

(3) When you are young there are many situations that occur that can make it very difficult for you to make friends and maintain the relationships at a level you desire. Are there any barriers set up by circumstances outside your control?

Example: You live in a bedsit and are not allowed visitors.

Task 4 (on your own or in small groups)

How honest are you?

(1) One of your closest friends tells you he's won a short story competition. You are surprised as you had no idea he'd entered but also disappointed because you had entered yourself (but your friend does not know this). Do you:

    (a) Say you are pleased for him but are disappointed because you entered the same competition.

    (b) Congratulate him quietly and then change the subject.

(2) Your friend has passed her driving test first time round. Yours is tomorrow but you haven't told anyone because you don't feel confident about passing. Do you:

    (a) Congratulate her and say you've got yours in the morning but feel really nervous about it.

    (b) Congratulate her but decide only to tell her about the test if you pass.

(3) Your friend is always smartly dressed when you go out and is adventurous with colour and style. You have no idea about dress sense and often try to copy what your friend wears. Do you:

    (a) Admit to trying to copy, saying you realise it probably irritates her. Ask if she could help you choose clothes to suit your own colouring and personality as you so much admire her dress sense.

    (b) Continue to copy your friend, pretending that your new clothes had been bought some time ago.

(4) Your friend is good at a subject you have great difficulty with. Do you:

    (a) Struggle on, getting poor marks, hiding your homework and exam results.

    (b) Ask your friend for help, admitting your problems.

Task 4 continued

(5)   You walk off in a huff because your friends are making fun of the team you support. When they question you the next day about it, you:

    (a)   Say that they were making fun of your favourite team and felt they were making fun of you too for liking that team.

    (b)   Say nothing was wrong, you just had to go or you'd have missed your bus.

(6)   Your friends are arranging a trip to Alton Towers and ask you to come. You are terrified of Roller Coasters and Big Wheels – you nearly fell out of one when you were younger. Do you:

    (a)   Agree to go but plan to be ill on the day.

    (b)   Say thanks for the invite but you can't bear big fair rides.

(7)   Your interviewer is looking for someone who can use a word-processor. You need the job but know little about computers. Do you:

    (a)   Say you can use a word-processor and hope that once you've got the job someone will help you out.

    (b)   Say you have used a word-processor but have not had the chance to develop your skills. However, you'd love to learn and would be willing to stay after work to get to grips with it.

Task 5 (on your own or in small groups)

How open are you?

(1) A letter arrived addressed to you while you are at college. When you get home you find your mum has opened it and this upsets you. Do you:

    (a) Say you want to open your own mail in future and that your mum would have been angry if you'd opened one of her letters.

    (b) Snatch the letter from her and go away and sulk.

(2) Someone you work with has parents who are going through a divorce. Your parents divorced two years ago and you went through a hard time so you know this person must be suffering. Do you:

    (a) Look embarrassed as you ask her if she's all right.

    (b) Say: 'I know your parents are divorcing and you must be feeling dreadful. It's taken me a long time to get used to things – mine divorced two years ago.'

(3) You entered a friend for a squash competition as you know he plays well. But your friend is angry that you did it without asking him. Do you:

    (a) Say: 'OK, I won't do it again', then leave feeling resentful that he wasn't grateful.

    (b) Say, sorry, you realise now you should have told him about it. You'd thought he'd be keen and enjoy the challenge. You hadn't meant to upset him.

(4) Your friend makes an unkind comment on some aspect of your appearance that you have no control over. Do you:

    (a) Say that you feel hurt by the comment and wonder why it was said at all.

    (b) Shrug, feel resentful and become moody for the rest of the day.

Task 5 continued

(5) Your best friend does very well in exams and is also very good at sports. His confidence makes you feel inadequate and inferior. Do you:

    (a) Explain that some things he does makes you feel small and give examples.

    (b) Stay silent each time you are made to feel bad about yourself.

(6) Your friend forgets your birthday. Do you:

    (a) Become moody, feeling miserable about being forgotten but do not say why.

    (b) Say jokingly that he forgot your birthday and hope that if you ever forget his, he'll forgive you too.

(7) You took a GCSE at evening class and failed. You worked very hard for it and had felt sure you'd pass. You are disappointed and angry. Your boss asks why you are snapping at people today. Do you:

    (a) Say sorry, you didn't realise you were.

    (b) Say sorry. You had some bad news and weren't taking it very well.

Barriers in Friendships

Task 2

- It would be wrong to tease or to tell everyone – unless you want an enemy.

- If you keep quiet, etc., they won't feel embarrassed in front of you. If they find out you know they will respect you for not telling. But this is unlikely to make you their friend since, the chances are, they'll never know of your kindness.

- To have a quiet word – this option is most likely to make them your friend if they wanted to confide their problem but it involves an element of risk. It is a matter of judgement with the individuals involved whether they may resent this.

Task 3

(3) *Are there any barriers set up by circumstances outside your control?*

Suggestions:

(1) You are not allowed to take friends home because:

(a)   your parents are very strict

(b)   one parent is very ill

(c)   your parents are very intolerant of guests

(d)   one parent suffers from obsessive compulsive disorder and cannot bear others coming into the house ('to contaminate it')

(e)   your parents disapprove of your friends

(f)   your parents are intolerant of other races/cultures.

(2) You are too ashamed to take friends home because of:

(a)   your living conditions

(b)   your parents' behaviour

(c)   a parent is obviously an alcoholic or on drugs

(d)   a parent is very aggressive and unpredictable

(e) you are abused at home and don't feel comfortable about taking friends there.

(3) You are too embarrassed because:

(a) your family are far more wealthy than those of your friends

(b) your parents are eccentric

(c) a parent regularly has different sexual partners to stay

(d) your religion and culture are so different to your friends' and you don't want them talking about you behind your back.

(4) You are not allowed out without your parents so cannot meet friends out of college – for example, some cultures do not allow girls out without a chaperone or out late. Or your parents only allow you out with friends they approve of and when they know these friends' parents.

(5) You are not allowed to go to college functions such as parties and discos.

(6) Your parents restrict your money so that you cannot afford to go anywhere or to buy clothes suitable for 'going out'. And they do not allow you to get a job – in other words, they are strictly controlling you.

Task 4

The more honest answers are: 1a, 2a, 3a, 4b, 5a, 6b, 7b.

Task 5

The more open answers are: 1a, 2b, 3b, 4a, 5a, 6b, 7b.

Conclusion

Friends are important for mutual support and good mental health. Ideally, we should have a wide and varied social network to experience the full spectrum of friendships from the casual acquaintance to the intimate partner or best friend.

First impressions are important when we meet new people as they form the basis on which we may be judged. They can be the deciding factor on whether or not the person we meet is willing to invest time and effort in getting to know us better.

Recognise your strengths and weaknesses and the patterns of why certain relationships failed or never developed at all, even when that was what was desired. Use failed relationships as a valuable learning experience so that mistakes are not repeated.

When dealing with others, be genuine. It is common to hide aspects of your past so that private events do not come under the scrutiny of an unsympathetic person, but never revealing any part of yourself prevents a relationship from developing. Also, do not pretend to be anyone other than yourself.

Part 2

Introduction: Social skills training

Some people have picked up social skills throughout their life, being aware of verbal and non-verbal (body language) signals as they grew up and by having rewarding experiences when they got something right, for example, making new friends and keeping them. For others it is much harder and we cannot visualise how we appear to other people without the aid of someone telling us or showing us (such as with the aid of a camcorder).

Part Two deals with difficulties people have in social situations and considers social skills and how to acquire them. Role plays are performed to experience what it feels like to behave in a variety of positive and negative ways, to understand the difference between good social practice and inadequate social practice and to recognise how our own behaviour changes in response to others and how other's behaviour changes in response to ours.

Social and Relationship Codes of Behaviour

Social relationships have certain codes of behaviour. If we do not follow them we may risk becoming social outcasts. The code depends on the role we are playing, with whom we are dealing and where we are.

Task 1 (group discussion)

How would you expect the people listed below to behave?
Where would the interactions take place?

- Mother/daughter or father/son
- Wife/husband
- Boss/employee
- Partners, for example, boyfriend/girlfriend
- Pupil/teacher.

What might happen if the setting of the relationship changes? For example, meeting your boss for a meal instead of seeing her at work?

Codes of behaviour

We have different codes of behaviour, so that people can reach their goals in different relationships and in different settings. Not conforming to these codes may not be particularly important, whereas with others it might mean the break-up of a friendship.

Nimisha

Every time Alice met Nimisha, Nimisha complained. About her brothers, her mother, her bad health, the school meals, the teachers, the weather, the late buses, everything. Alice found some things inconvenient such as a bus being cancelled, but it was part of life and had to be accepted. Being with Nimisha made her feel gloomy and depressed.

Task 2 (group discussion)

For a relationship to work there should be some form of reward. Both people involved should obtain something good out of the relationship.

- Is Alice's relationship with Nimisha rewarding? (Give reasons.)
- What might happen between them?
- Give examples of unrewarding relationships.
- What can you do to make sure the cost of someone being friendly with you isn't too high?

Task 3 (group discussion)

Can you think of any other codes of behaviour in relationships?

Social and Relationship Codes of Behaviour

'Roles'

We all behave differently depending on the situation and who it is we are dealing with. If our behaviour does not match certain expectations, there may be difficulties with the relationship. For example, parents are expected to be caring – but if a mother or father regularly beats his/her children, this is not socially acceptable. It could mean children distrust and fear their parents and become emotionally withdrawn. It could also mean they distrust other people, which would then interfere with how they form their own friendships. The greatest risk is that the children perpetuate the cycle and beat their own children.

Task 1

How would you expect the people listed below to behave? Where would the interactions take place? These are merely suggestions – there are undoubtedly many points not included. I simply wish to give a starting point to discussions.

Mother/daughter or father/son

The parent is expected to be caring and supportive, listen to problems, not to abuse the child in any way (emotionally, psychologically or physically through neglect or punishment). The child is expected to stick to the house rules, help in the home, keep their room clean and tidy. Families are meant to share birthdays and important occasions, not to argue or shame one another in public. Such interactions would normally take place in the home.

Wife/husband

Each are meant to take on a fair share of household tasks, particularly if both work. Important decisions are expected to be made jointly. They should support one another and not ridicule each other in public. They are expected to show concern for one another, be loyal, keep confidences, remember birthdays and wedding anniversaries, regularly have sex with the other, be affectionate. These interactions would take place in the home.

Boss/employee

A boss is expected to take care of his/her staff by making sure they are in a safe place, have warmth and drinking facilities, regular breaks and holiday time and pay for work done. An employee is expected to turn up on time, work without making many mistakes, support the boss, be helpful and polite, dress appropriately. The interactions would take place at work.

Partners (e.g., boyfriend/girlfriend)

If you wish to start a romantic attachment, your behaviour would be more appropriate as that of an adult seeking the company of another adult, rather than that of a child seeking reassurance and security. Support should be two-way, otherwise the relationship is unbalanced. The interactions would take place at home, at school/work and in public.

Pupil/teacher

When you are with your friends you may speak and laugh loudly and use bad language, but when you enter a classroom with a teacher, you may become quiet and stop using bad language. Here, the teacher is the one in charge and organises the pupils. The pupil has to wait his turn or be given permission to speak in class. The pupil does what he's told. The interactions would take place in school.

What might happen if the setting of the relationship changes? For example, meeting your boss for a meal instead of seeing her at work?

> The relationship between a boss and employee is usually carried out at work — but if your boss asks you out to a pub or restaurant, the roles change — perhaps to a romantic attachment or sexual harassment.

> When dealing with members of our family, we expect to see them in the home. Outside the home the roles may change — for example, you may be very kind to a younger brother at home but when you are out shopping with your friends and are told to take him with you, you may not treat him nicely because you are embarrassed at being seen with him.

Task 2

Is Alice's relationship with Nimisha rewarding? (Give reasons.)

It is not rewarding because Nimisha is always demanding support and sympathy from Alice and does not give anything in return. She does not allow Alice to talk about her problems – she is only interested in herself. The relationship is unbalanced.

What might happen between them?

Alice may become very distant towards Nimisha and may avoid her. The friendship will not survive as people do not tend to stay in an unrewarding relationship (if the costs of the relationship outweigh the benefits then the relationship is likely to break down).

Give examples of unrewarding relationships.

- o When a friend never smiles or tells jokes or shows affection or rambles on about something which is not common to both.
- o In a couple where one partner is continually unfaithful or abusive.
- o Looking after an elderly or incapacitated person (although this relationship may continue because of moral obligations).
- o In a couple where one wants a child and the other does not – just being with the other person may not be enough to keep the relationship going.
- o In a family where a parent is an alcoholic and is all demanding and abusive.

(Usually a family relationship has to continue in some way – except in exceptional cases – but it is possible to reduce intimacy, frequency of contact or level of help, so limiting the rewards we give to others because of their behaviour.)

What can you do to make sure the cost of someone being friendly with you isn't too high?

We can limit the costs to others by reciprocating help given, listening to the other person when they show they wish to speak, supporting them when they need help, paying back borrowed money quickly, returning things borrowed, trying to make them happy, remembering that one good turn deserves another.

Task 3

Can you think of any other codes of behaviour in relationships?

Intimacy: Two people may not want the same level of intimacy – in which case one will pull back from the relationship (e.g., with two friends where one wants the relationship to become sexual). The same can happen if one person is not willing to have the same level of commitment (e.g., one wants to see the other only once a week, but the other wants to see them or talk to them on the phone every day.)

Codes of behaviour outside the relationship: Pairs of people do not exist in isolation so codes of behaviour are needed to deal with feelings of jealousy, for example, on keeping confidences and standing up for your friend when he/she is not around.

Loneliness and Poor Social Skills

Task 1 (group discussion)

Why are some people lonely?

Nimisha again

At home, Nimisha hears her mother complain about the price of food, the dirtiness of the streets, how Nimisha's homework is not good enough, how she must be a good girl to get a good husband, how no one can prepare food as well as her mother. Nimisha often wishes her mother stopped work when she came home to sit and listen about her day at school, her hopes and fears, her dreams of the future. But she never does. Nimisha also wishes she had more friends — even Alice who used to be her best friend was now avoiding her and she didn't know why.

Task 2 (group discussion)

1. Why do you think Nimisha has few friends?
2. What do you think she could do to make more friends or keep the ones she has?
3. Where did Nimisha learn her friendship/relationship skills?
4. What is Nimisha's relationship with her mother like?
5. What could Nimisha do to improve her relationship with her mother?
6. What is meant by social skills?
7. Why do many people lack social skills?

Task 3 (in one or several smaller groups)

Give as many examples of how someone lacking in social skills might behave. (You have probably behaved in this way or you might know someone who has!)

Task 4 (role play)

People lacking in social skills can be either confident or lacking in confidence. This may be manifested in many different ways. In groups, or with the class as a whole, act out conversations in pairs while the rest of the group/class observe. (Use the information gathered in Task 3 to re-enact scenes of possible social incompetence. Exaggerate the point if necessary.) Social skills training can help improve this kind of behaviour.

Loneliness and Poor Social Skills

Task 1

Why are some people lonely?

- People are often lonely because they are divorced or widowed or old or because they are set apart from those around them by having too little or too much money or from a different social background to the people they come across (someone who goes to the pub for entertainment may feel uncomfortable being invited to a formal dinner at a posh hotel for the first time in their lives).

- They can also be set apart from others by being different in other ways such as by being blind, disabled, ill or unemployed or from a different culture to the majority – in fact in any way which makes them a minority (the only one or nearly so).

- Someone who is lacking in social skills may also become very lonely.

Task 2

(1) *Why do you think Nimisha has few friends?*

- Perhaps she drives them away by being glum, complaining or generally behaving like her mother. She is not a rewarding person.

(2) *What do you think she could do make more friends or keep the ones she has?*

- Try to stop complaining, by saying more positive things, by rewarding her friends with big smiles when she sees them, by listening to them for a change, by asking them what is wrong (e.g. by asking Alice why she is avoiding her) and offering to put things right.

(3) *Where did Nimisha learn her friendship/relationship skills?*

- From her mother (and perhaps from other members of her family).

(4) *What is Nimisha's relationship with her mother like?*

- It is not rewarding – Nimisha's mother does to her what Nimisha did to Alice. There is poor communication – her mother talks at her, there is no conversation that involves listening and replying for both of them.

(5)   What could Nimisha do to improve the relationship with her mother?

    o She could ask her mother to stop what she is doing for a moment because she has something important to say. Nimisha could offer to help her mother when she needs it so that she doesn't find everyday chores so hard. Nimisha could point out to her mother that she needn't worry all the time about her work, because she always does her best and perhaps they could talk about the nice things that have happened to them during the day.

(6)   What is meant by social skills?

    o Social skills are the skills used in communicating with others in a constructive manner. (Knowing how to behave in certain social situations.)

    o Certain skills may help you to interact more constructively with other people. (For example, knowing how to be a supportive boss.) Such skills may be employed in order to make a relationship more rewarding.

(7)   Why do many people lack social skills?

    o They may not have been lucky enough to have good role models to follow in the home; or they may not have observed and then put into practice such behaviour. It may be that they are isolated for some reason and so are not used to meeting people, or that they are desperately shy.

Task 3

Task 3 contains information from page 94 of *Social Networks and Social Influences in Adolescence* by John Cotterell (1996) published by Routledge and reproduced with permission.

Give as many examples of how someone lacking in social skills might behave. (You have probably behaved in this way or you might know someone who has!)

Those who experience social failure have been shown to:

    o Have conversational difficulties – such as, in starting conversation, discussing personal matters or making appropriate kinds of self-disclosure (it may be inappropriate to tell a complete stranger about intimate details of your life as they will feel embarrassed, or to describe in detail an operation you had as it may bore them).

    o Be unable to adjust the amount of information to their listener's interest, or discussing topics so generally that the listener is unsure of the point being made, or is unable to make sense out of what is being said.

    o Be less talkative and ask fewer questions – unable to ask about the other person's problems or interests – for fear of rejection, that it is not their business or that they don't know the other person well enough. Unable to recognise that the other person's point of view might be different and ask them about it.

o Be self-focused (introspective) – concerned with their own problems.

o Fail to give out non-verbal clues, for example, when they are going to start talking (to stop both parties talking at the same time), not making it clear when the subject is closed (continues discussion after a long pause as though no time had elapsed).

o Have a self-blaming style that is intolerant of their own faults – makes them vulnerable to doubts and lack of confidence.

o Have little variety in what they talk about and no sense of humour.

o Have a judgemental attitude that prevents them from seeing the other person's point of view. Since they are not open to new ideas, their personal growth is hindered.

SESSION 10
Speech and Body Messages

Tariq

Tariq, glancing at the floor, told his girlfriend, 'I love you'. He spoke in a flat voice, his tone never changing. He could have been talking about the weather, Preeti thought. Did Tariq really mean what he'd said?

Task 1 (group discussion)
• Why did Preeti wonder whether Tariq really loved her? • How should Tariq have sounded? • How should Tariq have behaved to convince Preeti he loved her?

Speech messages

These are the voice changes we use to make what we say more meaningful:

- **Volume** – we shout if we are angry but not if we are in public having a private chat. Whispering is not part of normal conversation as no one would be able to hear you.

- **Speed** – drawling may show boredom or be used as a put-down (to make someone feel small); speaking quickly can show excitement.

- **Emphasis** – for example, **I** was very upset. I **was** very upset. I was **very** upset. I was **upset**. Each sentence here has a slightly different meaning.

- **Tone** – this can be warm and round with a deep timbre (good for showing strong emotions) or shrill and thin (to show excitement or anxiety).

- **Pronunciation** – clearly pronounced words help you to be easily understood, mumbled or slurred speech does not.
- **Accent** – this can give information on where you come from and your social background.
- **Firmness** – whether you can talk assertively when necessary.
- **Use of pauses and silences** – can be used to give effect to your words or to change the subject. Too much pausing may indicate confusion or lack of confidence.

Body messages

These are messages given through body language which include:

- **Facial expression** – shows happiness, interest, surprise, fear, sadness, anger, disgust.
- **Gaze and eye contact** – looking the other person in the face shows interest. You can also see their expression and know a bit about what they are thinking and feeling.
- **Gestures** – nodding the head to agree or shaking it to disagree, pointing, clenching a fist, using rude gestures.
- **Posture** – confident people walk upright. It is friendly to crouch down to speak to a child so that eyes are at the same level and to turn your body towards the person you are talking to. Leaning forward shows you are interested in what the person has to say.
- **Physical distance** – for close friends, lovers and relatives you can sit or stand very close to someone. But with less close friends and at social gatherings the gap is wider. For strangers, shopkeepers and for people not known at all well the gap is wider still. Distance is also used to start and finish conversations – you move closer to someone when you wish to say something and move away when you have finished your conversation.

Recognising speech and body messages

Tasks 2–6 (role play: group)

- Two students are to act a breakfast scene.
- One student uses speech and body messages that imply something about the other. But they must not use the actual word they are trying to get across.
- The 'other' has to guess what that message or word is.
- Students watching must also try to guess what the word or message is.
- Different pairs may act the different messages.

Discussion after each role play:
- How were the messages put across?
- Were the messages clear? (Did everyone guess the message?)
- Could the messages have been improved? (If so, how?)
- Were both speech and body messages given?

Speech and Body Messages

The background and Task 1 of this session are based on information obtained from pages 60–65 of *Human Relationship Skills* by Professor Richard Nelson-Jones (1990) reproduced with the permission of Cassell plc, Wellington House, 125 Strand, London, England.

Task I

Why did Preeti wonder whether Tariq really loved her?

- o He did not look her in the eye – people tend to avoid the eyes when they are lying, and his voice sounded flat – there was little emotion or feeling in his voice. Tariq did not give Preeti the body and speech messages to back up what he said.

How could Tariq have sounded?

- o Tariq could have said, 'I love you', quietly and endearingly, expressing as much feeling as possible.

How could have Tariq behaved to convince Preeti he loved her?

- o Tariq could have really looked her in the eyes while he spoke, and showed her warmth and affection.

Tasks 2–6

The breakfast scene:

- o One person is already in the kitchen, eating or preparing their breakfast. The second person walks in – the one to receive the messages. The person who gives the messages must lead the conversation, the receiver must try to reply to comments and take on board any surprises.
- o The sender of the messages must never use the actual word of the message they are trying to give, for example, stupid.
- o The observers and message receiver are not to guess out loud what the message is but wait until the end. The receiver is to first be given the opportunity of saying what they felt the message was – it is important that the receivers are allowed to interpret the message for themselves.

Message 1: You are stupid

Suggested speech messages:

- Did you forget the time? You'll be late if you don't hurry.
- Why do you pour milk into the bowl before your cornflakes?
- Don't you worry that you might be late again? Don't you think about the consequences?
- Your boss must be very patient with his employees.
- Do you make a lot of mistakes at work?
- I'll explain how to use the answering machine tonight, when there's more time.

Suggested body messages:

- Slow, clear patronising voice – talks as though to someone who is slightly deaf or cannot speak the same language.
- Looks exasperated.
- Looks impatient.
- Sighs loudly.
- Raises eyes to the ceiling while sharply taking in breath as though a great deal of patience is needed.
- Voice hard and teacher-like.
- Irritated voice.

Message 2: You are lazy

Suggested speech messages:

- You've surfaced at last.
- You don't look very happy. Don't you feel well again?
- Are you going in to work today?
- Did you get round to finishing your work/project?
- If you're going to call the taxi you'd better do it now. They're busy in the rush hours.
- It's your turn to cook again. And I don't want another pizza delivery, I'm sick of them.

Suggested body messages:

- Checking your watch when the receiver of the messages comes in.
- Looks snooty.
- Patronising voice – talks as though to a child.

Message 3: You are a liar

Suggested verbal messages:

- I thought you said you would make the tea this morning?
- Didn't you have to be in work early this morning?
- Are you still going to do the shopping tonight? I don't want to be let down like last time.
- I've heard that before.
- My white shirt had a stain on it this morning. You promised not to borrow it again.
- You promised to clean the bath after you'd used it, but it was dirty this morning.

Suggested messages:

- Looks of disbelief.
- Raised eyebrows.
- Snorting through your nose.
- Looking askance.

Message 4: You don't smell very nice

Suggested speech messages:

- If you got up a bit earlier you'd have time for a quick shower. It does wonders for waking you up.
- I bought this lovely aromatherapy soap. Try it and see if you like it.
- I'm going to the chemist in my lunch hour as I've run out of anti-perspirant. I can't do without it as I sweat so much on the way to work. Do you want me to get you anything?
- I'd like to buy you some toilet water/aftershave for your birthday. Do you have a favourite make?

Suggested body messages:

- Sniffing.
- Rubbing your nostrils between knuckle and thumb.
- Standing as far away as possible.

Message 5: I love you

Suggested speech messages:

- How are you this morning? Has your headache gone?

- I know you've got a busy day ahead so I've made you breakfast and I've ironed your blouse.
- I hope your meeting goes well.
- What time will you be back tonight? I thought we might get a take-away and have a quiet evening together.
- Is there anything you'd particularly like for your birthday? I know it's early yet but I like to think ahead.
- Mm. Are you wearing your new perfume/aftershave? It's very nice.
- You look very smart as usual.

Suggested body messages:

- Open posture – arms spread out across the back of the chair if sitting or across the worktop if standing.
- Open expression, plenty of eye contact and smiles.
- Laughter, if appropriate.
- Showing affection (if you feel comfortable doing this).

Role Play: Social No-Nos
(Preparation and Practice)

Role play: group

Pairs of students must act out a scene where one person (Norm) tries to make friends with the other (Frank) who is a complete stranger. The rest of the group watch.

- Norm has good social skills. Frank does not.
- The actors are to use as many speech and body messages as they can to get their character across.
- It might be easier for comparisons of social skills if Norm is always played by the same person. If so, five different Franks are needed plus one person who plays Norm.

Help notes

For preparing the roles, each actor needs to be given a couple of students to help. Those acting out the roles need to understand their individual character so need to be coached by the leader and other members of the group. They need to practise reading the scripts with meaning, using the speech and body messages written on the scripts and adding a few of their own where possible.

Frank's Descriptions

Confident person 1 (Know-All)

You are a very confident person and you like to sum up the people you talk to by staring at them, considering how they look and watching their expressions. You like to look them over as though they are objects of interest rather than people with feelings.

You are in no hurry to answer any questions put to you. When you are speaking you don't pause to let the conversation pass over to the other person. You are convinced that you have a wealth of knowledge and experience this other person can only dream of. You are doing the other person a service by talking to them – you are of superior intellect, of superior social status and have superior thoughts and aims in life.

Your life is important whereas the other person's is not.

Confident person 2 (I've-Got-To-Be-Right)

You like to think that your judgements of people are fair and well balanced. Although you like to hear other people's point of view, it is nearly always wrong and you feel it is your duty to tell them so.

You ask the other person a question or their opinion on something and then strongly disagree, giving every possible reason you can think of. Should the other person not agree with your comments, you do not let them finish what they have to say but interrupt at every opportunity, try to finish the other person's sentences for them or give advice when it is not appropriate (e.g. on something you have had no experience of and the other person has, or on something you cannot admit to knowing nothing about).

You assume you have all the answers and that they are superior to the other person's. You are not aware of the other's feelings and do not read any body language feedback.

You like to dominate others, have no fear of treading on the other's toes or of offending them. You are out to make an impression and to show people how good you are at conversation. You are unable to show any warm or friendly feelings.

Confident person 3 (I'm-Better-Than-Anyone)

You feel you are so superior to anyone else that you assume an air of boredom in conversation as though you really cannot be bothered to answer. After all, the rest of the world is full of people who are really not very clever.

You do not listen to the other person attentively and you are easily distracted. You avoid looking in the person's eye and prefer to look around the room or through the other person as though they do not exist rather than focusing on what the other has to say.

If you do deign to answer, you drawl the words as though it is a great effort even to be slightly civil to another person. You are the most important being in the world.

Confident person 4 (I-Want-To-Know-All-About-You)

You like to dominate a conversation but do not have a wide range of topics you are able to discuss, so start conversations by asking a series of questions about the other person's family life, love life, details of sexuality, earnings or their parents' earnings, where they live, how big the house is, what they do in their spare time, how many brothers and sisters and pets they have, and so on.

You have little of interest in your own life to focus on and you want to know how others are doing compared to you.

You do not give the other person a chance to ask questions and you won't allow room for one topic to develop naturally and equally between the two of you. If you get your teeth into something interesting you won't let the topic go. You ask more and more questions and delve more deeply.

If the other person is rude to you because of your questions, you feel very offended, say you were only making conversation and feel quite aggressive towards the other person for having the cheek to criticise your attempts at friendship.

Timid person (I'd-Prefer-Not-To-Be-Noticed)

You feel awkward in any social situation and avoid the other person's eye. You talk only if absolutely necessary and then you mumble – including greetings.

If possible, you sit or stand facing the other way (or to one side) from the person who is trying to talk to you. It is hard work to get you talking at all. All the initiative (opening topics of conversation) comes from the other person.

Your replies to any questions are monosyllabic (yes, no) – you do not enlarge on anything and your voice is barely audible. You make the other person think that it is not worth the effort holding a conversation with you.

You have no hope of reading body language because your eyes are forever downcast or covered by your hand.

Setting for the Role Play

The roles are acted out by a seaside café overlooking beautiful calm waters in a hot country where the characters are on holiday. The chairs face the sea and beach. Norm's hotel is within sight. Norm is already seated, then Frank arrives and takes a spare seat at the table.

Suggested character backgrounds

Norm is male. He is an engineering student on holiday because he won a competition. It is his first holiday abroad as his parents are not well off. He has been there two days when he meets Frank. Norm's girlfriend, Sal, is not around because she is ill in bed with a stomach bug, probably picked up from swimming in the sea. Norm has cut his leg and has a bandage on it. The cut had prevented him from following Sal into the water, hence his escape from the stomach bug. Norm is an only child and has been going out with Sal for about six months. They get on well but neither have ever considered marriage. Sal is also a student.

Frank is working in his Dad's computer firm and has good prospects of becoming a board member by the time he is thirty. He has been to this holiday resort twice before. The first time was with his parents and they made friends with another family there. This family have now retired there and have invited Frank to lunch the day he meets Norm. Frank is on holiday alone – he and his parents take separate holidays now that he is grown up – but he knows that whenever he is at a loose end, he will be welcome at his parents' friends' house. He has a brother but does not get on well with him.

Please note: although I have described Frank and Norm as male, this role play can be adapted for members of either sex to act out.

Scene for Confident Person 1 (Know-All)

Frank: Is this seat taken? (You don't wait for an answer before you sit down. As you sit, you stare at Norm and study Norm's clothes. Then you stare out to sea.)

Norm: Great isn't it? (You flash a brief smile at Frank.)

Frank: Yes. The Mediterranean always is, especially in June.

Norm: This is the life, sunning oneself by a beautiful sea. (You stretch your arms and put them behind your head so that you sit in a relaxed posture.) Been here long?

Frank: A week. (Snooty voice.) It's not my first visit, though.

Norm: I wish I could come every year. This is my first trip abroad.

Frank: (You turn to look Norm over again, raising an eyebrow.) My parents have always taken us abroad. It's not just the climate. It's the experience too. Does wonders for experiencing other cultures. My father says what's the use of having money, if you don't spend it. You should try to go away every year. See as many countries as you can.

Norm: Are you here with your parents then?

Frank: Oh no, I go on holiday by myself now. Have done for years. They like to do their thing and I like to do mine. (Talk while examining your fingers.)

Norm: You must have a good job.

Frank: Pretty good, I suppose. I hope to be on the board in my Dad's firm by the time I'm thirty. I learn quickly and I'm not afraid of hard work. (You look down your nose at Norm as though he is afraid of hard work.)

Norm:	(You open your mouth to ask what he does but he tells you before you get the chance. You relax back in your chair as the opportunity to speak has been lost.)

Norm: (You open your mouth to ask what he does but he tells you before you get the chance. You relax back in your chair as the opportunity to speak has been lost.)

Frank: We are one of the leading producers of computer software and hardware. As well as designing the latest chips – which are getting smaller and smaller – our programmers have developed games and educational packages. You've probably used some of our stuff in your school. Most have them. They are supposed to be more user friendly than our competitors' products. The labs where they make the chips are an eye opener. The atmosphere has to be clean and dust free to make perfect chips. Our quality control have very strict tests to check whether the chip is good enough to be passed. (You look out to sea rather than at Norm's face.)

Norm: (You open your mouth and lean forward to say what you do but you are interrupted again.)

Frank: Some of the bigger companies, of course, get much of their business through being so well known, so we have to fight against that, but once we've got customers we don't lose them because our products and services are so good. Our aftercare on all the PCs is excellent.

Norm: (Quickly, while you have the chance, you say...) I came with a friend. She's ill.

Frank: What's wrong with her? (You look a bit worried – it might be catching.)

Norm: Stomach bug.

Frank: Ah. Food poisoning? If ice cream has melted once and then been re-frozen, small icicles form, which you can see. A sure sign it hasn't been kept as it should have been. And with cold meats, even if they've been thoroughly cooked they can still get contaminated by raw meat, if they aren't kept separately in the fridge or if they aren't careful in the kitchens. You know, twenty per cent of the beef in the UK is contaminated with nasty E. Coli bugs. Best to only eat food that's piping hot or out of a packet or food that's been prepared away from meat, like bread in bakeries.

Norm: I don't think she got sick from the food. We ate more or less the same thing last night.

Frank: Ice cubes can make you sick if they are made out of contaminated water. Best to drink from cans or bottles – not out of a glass in case that's not clean – unless you're sure. You could always drink from a straw. That would stop you catching any nasty germs. Best still, don't eat in the same place again in case you get ill next time. (Looks at watch.) Got to go. Bye. (Leaves with the briefest of glances in Norm's direction.)

Norm: Bye.

Scene for Confident Person 2 (I've-Got-To-Be-Right)

Frank:	Is this seat taken? (You don't wait for an answer before you sit down. As you sit, you stare at Norm and study Norm's clothes.)
Norm:	Great here, isn't it?
Frank:	I like it. I've been before. It's nice to come back to.
Norm:	I wish I could have holidays like this every year.
Frank:	(Laughing…) You'll have to change your job then. Holidays cost money.
Norm:	Did you come with anyone?
Frank:	No. But my parents' friends are close by so I can go there when I'm bored of my own company.
Norm:	I came with a friend but she's ill. Stomach bug.
Frank:	What do you think that's from?
Norm:	She swallowed a lot of water yesterday when she swam in the sea. I guess it was dirty.
Frank:	It's much more likely to be from food. Did you eat different things?
Norm:	Mostly. I'm fine. I'm sure it was the water.
Frank:	It only takes one thing to be contaminated to make someone ill. Remember that E. Coli bug that struck down all those people in Scotland? That was from the meat. Did you eat the same meat?
Norm:	Yes. The only thing we ate that was different was the dessert. I had cake and she had ice cream.
Frank:	That would be it then. They've probably not kept it cold enough. Especially if it was out on display all evening and

	every evening. Was it a buffet type meal where you chose from the counter?
Norm:	It was, but…
Frank:	Were there icicles in the ice cream? I saw this programme where researchers went to these restaurants in Spain and chose food from the counter, took it to their tables and put it in plastic bags. Then the bags were labelled, put into a cool box and sent away for analysis. The ice cream was one of the worst things for all the bacteria found in them.
Norm:	I didn't see any ice bits in it. Sal never complained, but…
Frank:	Probably too dark. That's why they don't have bright lights in these places.
Norm:	I'm sure it was from the sea. I didn't go in because I'd cut my knee badly on some glass.
Frank:	If I were you, I'd eat somewhere else tonight.
Norm:	(Sigh. You give up.)
Frank:	Well, must go. I'm expected for lunch in ten minutes.
Norm:	Bye. (Heave a sigh of relief.)

Scene for Confident Person 3 (I'm-Better-Than-Anyone)

Frank:	(You just sit down without asking permission.)
Norm:	Isn't it great here?
Frank:	To what are you referring? The weather, the view or the fact that you're on holiday? (Doesn't look at Norm, looks out to sea.)
Norm:	All of those, I suppose. (Surprise at Frank's manner.)
Frank:	(Raises eyebrows. Doesn't Norm know?)
Norm:	(Longish silence.) Been here long?
Frank:	(Sighs.) I've only just arrived. (Looks past Norm, avoiding his eye.)
Norm:	I meant, (slightly annoyed) have you been on holiday long?
Frank:	(Painfully, you say…) A week. (Concentrating on a passer-by and following her progress.)
Norm:	I came the day before yesterday. With a friend. She's ill.
Frank:	Really. (Not said as a question. Just exasperated annoyance.)
Norm:	(Longish silence.) Are you staying at the hotel? (Points across the road, to the other side.)
Frank:	No. (Looks straight past Norm as though Norm's not there.)
Norm:	I am. It's quite nice but I've not had much to compare it with. I've never been in a hotel before. This is my first time abroad, in fact.
Frank:	Really. (Sounds bored.)
Norm:	(Sighs and just admires the view.)
Frank:	(A few moments later Frank gets up and walks off, without looking at Norm.)

Scene for Confident Person 4 (I-Want-To-Know-All-About-You)

Frank: Is this seat taken?

Norm: Help yourself. (Later…) It's great here isn't it?

Frank: Oh, yes. I just love the sea and sun. I've been here twice before but I still love it. On holiday?

Norm: Yes, we arrived the day before yesterday.

Frank: Who did you come with? Your girlfriend? (Stares intently at Norm.)

Norm: Yes.

Frank: How long have you been together? (Stares intently at Norm.)

Norm: About six months.

Frank: That's nice. Do you think you'll get married? (Stares intently at Norm.)

Norm: (Laugh, embarrassed.) I don't know.

Frank: You're not very close then? (Stares intently at Norm.)

Norm: I wouldn't say that. We've not thought about it really. (Voice a bit cold and awkward.)

Frank: Where are you staying?

Norm: That hotel over there. (Points.)

Frank: Are you sharing rooms or have you got separate rooms?

Norm: (Embarrassed pause – you don't want to be rude to the other person, but Frank's too nosy for your comfort.) We're sharing.

Frank: What are the rooms like? (Stares intently at Norm.)

Norm: What do you mean? (Defensive. Is Frank going to ask about the sleeping arrangements?)

Frank:	Do you have a bathroom or a balcony?
Norm:	Oh, it's en suite. We're the wrong side for a balcony. Where are you staying? (Very quickly so that Frank can't get another question in.)
Frank:	In a small hotel round the corner. Have you been on holiday before with your girlfriend or is this your first time away together?
Norm:	It's my first time away with anyone.
Frank:	Didn't you go on holidays with your family?
Norm:	No they didn't have the money. How about you? (Quickly so that Frank can't ask a question.)
Frank:	I've been away with my family a lot. Now they do their thing and I do mine. So how come you're here now? Have you got a good job?
Norm:	I don't work, I'm a student.
Frank:	Did your girlfriend pay for the holiday?
Norm:	No, I...
Frank:	What does your girlfriend do?
Norm:	She's a student too.
Frank:	All right for some. (Disparaging laugh.)
Norm:	What do you mean?
Frank:	Well, others go out to work to earn their keep.
Norm:	(Bristling...) That's the idea, when I'm trained for my chosen career.
Frank:	What's that?
Norm:	(Irritated...) Engineering.
Frank:	So how come you can afford to come here? It must have been quite expensive.
Norm:	I won the holiday in a competition.
Frank:	What sort of competition? (Stares.)
Norm:	(In a jokey voice...) Is this a hundred questions?

Frank: (Affronted.) Well, I'm just making conversation. Pardon me for talking to you.

Norm: (Embarrassed silence.) I'm sorry, I didn't mean to sound rude...

Frank: (Looks at watch.) Well, I must be going... (Leaves without looking at Norm.)

Scene for Timid Person
(I'd-Prefer-Not-To-Be-Noticed)

Frank: Excuse me, is this seat taken? (You wait patiently for the answer and then sit down.)

Norm: Great here isn't it?

Frank: I'm sorry? (Nervously looking quickly at Norm and then away.)

Norm: I said, it's great here isn't it?

Frank: Yes, lovely. (Lots of nods but you avoid Norm's eye. You concentrate on the view and the people walking by, hoping Norm will not speak to you again.)

Norm: Have you been here long?

Frank: Erm, about a week. (Flash a nervous smile and look away again.)

Norm: I arrived the day before yesterday.

Frank: (Nods vaguely while looking at the sea.)

Norm: Are you here on your own?

Frank: (Looks even more nervous and would prefer not to answer.) Yes. (Barely audible.)

Norm: I came with a friend but she's ill.

Frank: (Silence.)

Norm: She caught a stomach bug.

Frank: (Silence.)

Norm: This is my first time abroad. My parents couldn't afford holidays when I was a child.

Frank: (Silence.)

Norm: Are you staying at the hotel? (Points.)

Frank: No.

Norm: With friends?

Frank: There's a hotel round the corner.

Norm: Is it nice?

Frank: Yes.

Norm: I like mine but I've nothing to compare it with. It's the first I've ever stayed in.

Frank: Oh. (Examines nails and fingers, avoiding Norm's eye.)

Norm: How long are you here for?

Frank: Another week.

Norm: Aren't you lonely on your own?

Frank: (Looking very uncomfortable, shifting in chair, examining feet and looking anywhere except in Norm's direction.) No.

Norm: (Leans back in chair to admire the view.)

Frank: (Shifts around uncomfortably in chair and eventually moves away without a word or look.)

Role Plays in Action

Act out the prepared role plays in order.

Task 1 (group discussion)

After each role play discuss how you felt about Frank and Norm.
How well did their conversation go?

Task 2 (group discussion)

What particular problems does a confident person with poor
social skills have?

Task 3 (in groups)

Have a volunteer act out, with Norm, someone with good social
skills, in other words, someone who is socially adept. (See
Student Help Sheet 7.)

Or: the group could write the scene for the socially adept
person, remembering to avoid the mistakes of the roles just
played. Then someone could act it out with Norm.

What made this role play successful? Are there any ideas you
can pick up to use in your own life? (Are you doing these things
already or is there room for improvement?)

Task 4 (group discussion)

How do people behave when:

- They want to be chatted up by someone.
- They don't want to be chatted up by someone.

How can flirting help?

Role Plays in Action

Task 1: Possible questions to discuss depending on the group ability

- o What holds back the friendship between Norm and Frank?
- o What is off-putting in Frank's behaviour?
- o How would you react if you were Norm?
- o Describe Frank's character.
- o Did the conversation bring the characters closer or drive them apart?
- o Were there any signs of true 'friendship'?

Further possible questions after all the role plays:

- o Which character got the most information from Norm? Does this show how well the relationship is developing?
- o What personal information did you get from each character?

Analysis of role play scenes

Confident person 1

Frank does not pick up on cues to find out more about Norm. If he does acknowledge something Norm says, it's to put him down (raising an eyebrow when Norm says it is his first trip abroad) or to worry over whether Sal's illness is infectious or not.

Frank rarely makes eye contact even when talking to Norm and deliberately sets himself apart from Norm by boasting and highlighting the differences between them rather than picking out any similarities. Frank also implies (with no prior knowledge to back him up) that Norm is lazy.

Once Frank has chosen his topic of conversation (himself and his job) he allows no interruption from Norm, ignores any cues to hand the conversation over and bores Norm with details. He has not rewarded Norm in any way, for example, by giving him a share in the conversation and he learns absolutely nothing about how Norm came to be on holiday or very little else. Frank has divulged all the information and has given all the opinions.

There is no warmth in Frank's farewell or acknowledgement that it was pleasant talking to Norm or that it was worth the effort investing time talking to him.

Confident person 2

Frank does not respect Norm's opinions or try to find out why Norm has them. Frank likes to interrupt and his opinions are sacred – he knows he is right. The conversation didn't flow at all. Once Frank had picked a topic, he had to show Norm that he knew all about it. Frank probably thought he was doing Norm a favour by telling him all those interesting things, assuming Norm knows nothing about food poisoning. Frank ignored all but one type of cue from Norm and that was about Sal being ill. There was no interest shown in anything else Norm might have to say. Frank was too full of himself.

Confident person 3

Frank deliberately picks on points that are not worth elaborating. He is so caught up in the precision of words that the whole point of making any conversation is lost on him.

Frank shows no desire to communicate and makes it obvious that he resents Norm's questions – he considers them an intrusion in his nice peaceful world. Frank thinks he is better than Norm and is proud of the fact he does not tolerate stupid people making small talk. He is determined to invest as little as possible in the interaction and short of asking Norm outright to shut up and leave him alone he does the next best thing.

Confident person 4

Much is discussed with Frank interrogating Norm. Frank sees nothing wrong with monopolising the conversation to suit his own ends and does not feel obliged to volunteer similar information about himself. Frank's questions are far too personal on so brief an acquaintance and only make Norm retreat. Frank ignores all body language cues about Norm disliking this form of passing time (it is not a conversation as there isn't free, two-way communication) until Norm is forced to say something outright.

Frank failed to recognise the growing irritation in Norm's voice and his increasing reluctance to answer the questions. Once it is made clear to Frank that Norm has a problem, Frank becomes defensive and thinks that Norm dislikes him and is rejecting his friendship.

Timid person

Frank simply cannot think of anything to say. He doesn't even appear to be making the effort and his discomfort makes Norm feel uncomfortable. Frank ignores all the cues that Norm gives him and doesn't appear sufficiently interested in what Norm has to say, in order to ask a question. Norm gave Frank many openings and even supplied the answer to a possible question a number of times. Frank seems very ill at ease with his own company and is unable to smile at Norm, acknowledging the compliment he paid him by trying to start the conversation in the first place.

Task 2

Confident people with poor social skills are more likely to:

- o Monopolise conversations.
- o Interrupt when others are speaking to them.
- o Interrogate.
- o Be critical or disagree.
- o Make personal comments that are inappropriate.
- o Ignore (or fail to recognise) feedback from the other person, indicating that they should pass the conversation over or change the subject.

Task 3

Socially adept person

Plenty of rewarding smiles are given by Frank. He realises that conversations usually start by discussing something impersonal like the scenery. Small talk may be necessary to start a conversation with a stranger. The conversation soon passes naturally from one to the other with no pressure being put by Frank on Norm to answer personal questions. Any information/disclosures are given freely and easily. They seem very comfortable with each other's company and disclosures are balanced.

Frank respects Norm's thoughts on why Sal was ill and accepts his explanation after showing both sympathy and interest. Both Frank and Norm listen to what the other has to say and base their next comment or question on what they have heard. The conversation is not single-tracked, but touches upon several areas. Deeper probing may be left for the next encounter, if there is one.

Their leave-taking is pleasant with Frank offering his wishes for Sal, acknowledging Norm's concern. There is no pressure to meet up again, but there is a suggestion that they might since they found each other interesting, friendly and rewarding. This meeting may constitute the start of a new friendship.

Task 4

Suggestions

Wanting to be chatted up:

- o Plenty of smiles.
- o Frequent lowering of eyes (being coy or engagingly shy).
- o Looking at the person askance (a way of flirting).
- o Staring intently or adoringly into the other's eyes.
- o Blushing, when the other looks at you or asks a question.
- o Leaning forward to listen more closely to what the other has to say.
- o Not being afraid of physical contact.
- o Laughing.

Not wanting to be chatted up:

- o Not responding to questions
- o No eye contact.
- o Moving away.
- o Telling the other person to leave you alone.
- o Turning the front of your body away from the person.

Flirting is a natural way of expressing romantic interest in someone else.

Possible Scene for the Socially Adept

Frank: Is this seat taken? (You smile while waiting for a reply and then sit down.)

Norm: It's great here isn't it?

Frank: Lovely. This is my third visit. (Looks at Norm and then out to sea.)

Norm: Lucky you. It's the first time I've ever been abroad.

Frank: How come? (Looks interested and holds Norm's gaze while he asks the question.)

Norm: My parents didn't have the money. (Norm looks away and then back at Frank.)

Frank: And now you have? (Eye contact.)

Norm: (Smiles.) No. I won the holiday in a competition.

Frank: That was clever. I've never met anyone who won anything like that before. What sort of competition was it? (Eye contact, looks impressed.)

Norm: Just a tie breaker thing after answering a few questions. I only entered it for a laugh, I never expected to win. (Glances down shyly.)

Frank: Well done. (Smiles approvingly.) Someone obviously liked it. What do you do?

Norm: I'm a student. Engineering.

Frank: (Glances away.) A far cry from playing with words. (Makes eye contact again.) I'm in computers. I joined my Dad's firm, so it's been easy for me. Same with the holidays abroad.

Norm: Are you with anyone? (Eye contact.)

Frank: No. My parents and I prefer to take separate holidays now that I'm grown-up. If I had a girlfriend I would have brought her along. What about you? (Eye contact.)

Norm: I came with a friend. Unfortunately she's ill with a stomach bug.

Frank: What a shame. What do you think caused it? (Polite interest.)

Norm: She swam in the sea yesterday and swallowed a lot of water.

Frank: Would that give her a stomach bug? I thought it would be more likely to be food poisoning. (Looks out to sea and back again.)

Norm: I   don't think so because we ate more or less the same thing.

Frank: What did you eat that was different?

Norm: I had cake for dessert and she had ice cream. But I don't think it was that.

Frank: Why?

Norm: No one else in the hotel complained of being ill this morning and plenty of others had eaten ice cream.

Frank: Why didn't the sea make you ill then?

Norm: I didn't go in. I cut my leg badly on some glass. (Points to bandage.)

Frank: That was probably lucky then. Otherwise you'd be stuck in bed too.

Norm: (Laughs.) Probably. How long are you here for?

Frank: Another week. Friends of my parents live close by, so I can visit them when I tire of my own company. In fact, I've been invited there for lunch today.

Norm: Do they live here or are they on holiday too?

Frank: They've retired here. We met years ago when we first came on holiday and their children played with me and my brother.

Norm: It must be nice to have a sibling. I'm an only child.

Frank: (Smiling, confidingly.) It's not all fun and games with my brother. We clash so frequently that I've often wished I'd been an only child. (Looks at watch.) It's time I left. It wouldn't do to be late. (Smiles.) Perhaps I'll see you around?

Norm: (Smiles.) I shan't be going far. (Points to the bandaged leg.) It hurts like hell to walk on. Besides, it's not fair to leave Sal on her own for long.

Frank: Maybe see you tomorrow then. I often come here for the view. Hope she feels better.

Norm: Thanks. (Smiles.)

Frank: Bye. (Smiles and leaves.)

Norm: Bye.

SESSION 13

Self-Disclosure

Revealing your inner self may help you get close to another person — this is called self-disclosure. It means that you can turn to your friend when you are in need and vice versa. This is because there is more trust.

Self-disclosure can include telling thoughts, opinions, feelings, things that have happened to you and things you like and hate.

Task 1 (in one large or several smaller groups)

In the following cases, was it appropriate for the person to have self-disclosed. Why?

(1) Jane was standing at the bus stop, peering out into the fog looking for her bus when someone joined her in the queue. 'I can't stand much more of this,' Jane said, 'I'm late for my job interview.'

(2) Your new boss at work confides in you, 'My husband's leaving me for a married woman.'

(3) You are at a dinner party and the man sitting next to you tells you about his constipation.

(4) You've just made friends with someone at college and need someone to talk to. 'I'm really upset. My boyfriend wants me to have sex with him but I can't let him get close because I was sexually abused by my uncle. And I can't think about it because my Mum's left with our next door neighbour and my Dad's girlfriend is moving in. My brother's in trouble with the police for stealing a bike and my sister's sniffing glue.'

Task 1 continued

(5) You are on an Intercity train travelling to visit your grandmother. You are sitting next to someone you've never met before and find out that she's a single mother. You tell this complete stranger that you're worried sick because you think you might be pregnant (or that you think your girlfriend might be.)

(6) You sit next to the same person on the train every day on the way to college. You say hello to him and make a comment about the weather.

(7) You are pleased to see someone you met the night before in front of you in a queue. You smile and say, 'I passed my driving test this morning!'

Task 2 (in one large or several smaller groups)

Why do the following people make disclosures?

(1) Miranda openly tells people she is good at sports but not at maths and English. She prefers to be open about what she can and can't do so that she's not teased so much. Other, more private things, she chooses not to talk about.

(2) When something big happens in the news, Michael likes to talk about it with his friends so that he hears their points of view and compares theirs to his. Sometimes he changes his way of thinking because of his friends' ideas. Talking about the news helps him understand it better.

(3) Pete met someone at the squash courts he thought he'd like to know better. He smiled and said, 'Hi. I'm Pete.'

(4) Sally waited at the bus stop, bored. Then another woman came up and Sally shivered saying, 'It's so draughty in these shelters.'

(5) When Tania heard that Petra's Dad had died she went up to her and said how sorry she was, that she knew what it was like because her Dad had died last year.

Task 3 (group discussion)

What things in your own life have encouraged you to talk more about yourself? (Think of when other people are encouraged to self-disclose – real and fictional.) Does the setting have anything to do with how much you are prepared to tell? Some disclosures might be made to shock a parent or teacher, to gain attention or to get sympathy or to deliberately give a false impression. Relationships only develop into true friendships when friends are honest and genuine. People feel cheated if they find out they have been lied to or manipulated and once trust is lost, it is extremely hard to regain it. Value the other person's trust and respect and they will yours.

Self-disclosure

Task 1

In the following cases, was it appropriate for the person to have self-disclosed. Why?

1. Yes, it was appropriate for Jane to disclose. It wasn't very personal information and someone else who was waiting for the bus would be sympathetic about her dilemma. Talking about her interview, if a conversation developed, would take her mind off worrying so much and the person might be able to offer advice, for example, calling the company from a public telephone to explain why she was running late.

2. No, it was not right for the boss to disclose this, because it was very personal information and she barely knew her employee – it is more usual for this to happen with people who have worked together for a long time.

3. No, it was not appropriate for intimate and personal details to be discussed at the dinner table. (Also, they were not close friends.)

4. No, it was not appropriate to confide in, pouring out all your troubles to, someone you hardly know. Problems like this would be gradually revealed as you build up trust with another person. You do not know this person well enough to talk about such personal matters. If you so easily tell her everything, she may not trust you with her problems and so the friendship is not likely to develop.

5. Yes, it was appropriate to confide – talking in depth and for a long time to a complete stranger may sometimes be helpful if they have had similar experiences. There is no risk of gossip and this person might be able to help, by giving advice, or simply listening, or telling you about their experience, or giving a different view point from the one you have – as long as they are happy about being burdened with your troubles – in this case the person would understand as they went through it themselves.

6. Yes, it was appropriate to talk to the person about the weather – this is the way friendships start and you were not forcing closeness – talking about the weather to a stranger is socially acceptable.

7. Yes, it is appropriate to disclose this information – it is positive and allows the person to congratulate you and share your feelings of success. When you share negative information, on the other hand, you have to be more careful about who you disclose it to, because you may risk being made fun of or gossiped about.

Tasks 2 and 3 of this section contain information obtained from *Social Skills in Interpersonal Communication* by Owen Hargie, Christine Saunders and David Dickson (1994) published by Routledge and reproduced with permission.

Task 2

Why do the following people make disclosures?

1. To define herself. Miranda decides what she wants known about herself. It is better than her friends and acquaintances deciding for her and saying things about her that she doesn't want to hear.

2. To know himself better. Discussing ideas with someone else either confirms or changes them; Michael learns more about himself, his feelings and reasons for having them when he has to explain or justify them to someone else.

3. To encourage the other person to give their name in return – information is exchanged. It can lead to giving details of their jobs or about their interests. (Self-disclosure on a fairly casual and non-intimate level.) It is only through doing this that Peter can find out whether he has anything in common with the other person.

4. To open a conversation – to give a starting point on which to build if the other person wants to talk too.

5. To share the experience, to show she has something in common with Petra, to show sympathy and understanding, so developing closeness.

Task 3

What things in your own life have encouraged you to talk more about yourself? (Think of when other people are encouraged to self-disclose – real and fictional...)

- o   When you are anxious or having a crisis you tend to disclose more – also if you are an extrovert.
- o   If you have a sympathetic ear ready and waiting you are encouraged to disclose. Also if you trust the listener to keep what you say in confidence.
- o   One-off encounters (stranger on a train) encourages self-disclosure as your secrets are kept safe.

Does the setting have anything to do with how much you are prepared to tell?

- o   A warm atmosphere (comfortable chairs, gentle lighting) may encourage self-disclosures.
- o   With just one person to talk to, self-disclosures are more likely than in a group. (Privacy is important.)
- o   Prisoners sharing a cell with each other (or two people stuck in a lift for a long time) are more likely to have higher levels of self-disclosure.

Listening Skills

Being a good listener is an important social skill. Cutting a person off in conversation makes him feel small and worthless. If someone tells you that you have done something wrong, don't be too quick to deny it. Listen to what they have to say and their reasons why. It helps to know how others see you – then you have a chance of improving yourself. Trust is built from sharing disclosures and regularly listening to others. Listening to someone with a different set of life circumstances (e.g. rich/poor, old/young, boy/girl) can help you understand their point of view and their reasons for doing certain things. You can fill gaps in your understanding about people who are different to you.

Task 1 (in one large or several smaller groups)

What do you do when and what do you not do when:

(1) Your best friend moans about the course he's just started, saying it's boring. You'd warned him before he signed down for it.

(2) Your friend tells you she hates being so skinny.

(3) Your friend tells you he has a problem and needs to talk to you about it. You are feeling really ill and the last thing you want to do is listen to someone else's problems.

(4) Your friend wants you to help him choose who to vote for in the election. You are very politically active, have strong views and always follow the news.

Task 2: Role play (in groups)

(1) You need two volunteers to act the parts of a listener and speaker (someone with a problem). The rest of the group watch.

(2) The speaker needs to think of a problem (e.g. you got caught shoplifting or your parents have decided to divorce each other or you don't get on with your Mum/Dad).

(3) The speaker and listener must seat themselves as they think best to act out the parts. The listener must encourage the other person to talk.

(4) At the end of the role play, the other students comment on how it went. (Was the person a good listener? Did the listener get the other person to open up? How?)

Task 3 (in groups)

Make a list of 'Don'ts' for how a good listener should behave. (Remember that the speaker needs to find the experience rewarding.)

Listening skills

Task 1

What do you do when and what do you not do when:

1. Your best friend moans about the course he's just started, saying it's boring. You'd warned him before he signed down for it.

   Do: Ask about the course and what he finds particularly boring about it. Be sympathetic. Make sure you understand what he's feeling by saying, 'Do you mean…' to summarise what he's said.

   Don't: Say, 'I told you so.'

2. Your friend tells you she hates being so skinny.

   Do: Ask why. Say how nice she looks, that it suits her. Offer to help find out about how she can put on weight sensibly. Ask how she feels about herself. Respect her as a separate and unique person with a right to her own thoughts and feelings independent from your own.

   Don't: Say, 'Most people would love to look like you.' (Unsympathetic.) Or: 'I don't know why you're making such a fuss. There's nothing wrong with how you look.' (Saying your opinion is more important than how she sees herself.)

3. Your friend tells you he has a problem and needs to talk to you about it. You are feeling really ill and the last thing you want to do is listen to someone else's problems.

   Do: Explain you are feeling unwell and arrange a time to meet. Check that the problem can wait. (That your friend is not feeling suicidal or something really bad has happened in his family.) If the problem can't wait, say you'd love to help him right away.

   Don't: Say, 'I'm too ill to listen. Go away.' Or pretend to listen but repeatedly have to ask him what he means because you haven't been listening.

4. Your friend wants you to help him choose who to vote for in the election. You are very politically active, have strong views and always follow the news.

Do: Explain that you have very strong opinions on politics so would not necessarily be the best person to give him all round advice. You can only speak in favour of one political party.

Don't: Agree and then brainwash him with your set of values and ideals, putting down any differences of opinion.

Task 2: Role play

Sending good body messages

To show you are ready to listen: face the speaker with your whole body. Do not sit cross-legged or with your arms folded. Lean slightly forward and nod your head to show you are following what is being said. Make frequent eye contact and make appropriate facial expressions – in other words, looking interested, concerned, pleased for them. Briefly touching someone's arm or shoulder may help to show concern but only if it does not make them feel uncomfortable.

Sending good voice messages

Respond to what is said in a sufficiently loud, clear, firm, even and steady voice, emphasising your concerns to show understanding. Pause before contributing to check the speaker has reached the end of what she wants to say. Brief silences also allow time to think before speaking to make what is said more meaningful.

Using openers

Example: 'How was your day?' 'You look happy/sad.' 'What do you think about...?' encourage the person to talk. Show that you are ready to listen with your body language. Tell them to take their time. Show them that you listen to what they say by including every so often phrases like, 'Go on...', 'Oh...', 'I see...' in your conversation. Encourage the person to talk by an open question, such as 'What do you feel about...' rather than, 'Did you hate that?'

Rewording and reflecting feelings

Sum up what the speaker says and how she feels to show you understand what has been said.

Task 3 of this session is based on information obtained from pages 126–129 of *Human Relationship Skills* by Professor Richard Nelson-Jones (1990) reproduced with the permission of Cassell plc, Wellington House, 125 Strand, London, England.

Task 3: 'Don'ts' for good listening skills

It is your choice whether to follow this 'good listener's guide'. Some situations demand that these guide lines are not strictly adhered to. Others don't. (For example, you might be justifiably angry at someone and so express it by shouting.) Knowing the difference is an important skill.

- o Don't put the other person down when you listen to them.
- o Don't change the other person's chosen topic of conversation.
- o Don't be judgemental. ('You've messed up your life.')
- o Don't blame. ('It's all your fault.')
- o Don't get aggressive. (Shouting, calling names, belittling or putting down.)
- o Don't moralise or preach. ('Honesty is the best policy.')
- o Don't advise or teach. ('You need more exercise.')
- o Don't deny the other person's feelings. ('You shouldn't feel sorry for yourself.')
- o Don't talk inappropriately about yourself. ('You think you've got troubles. Mine are far worse…')
- o Don't interrogate by using questions to make the other feel threatened.
- o Don't reassure without good reason. ('You'll manage. I know you can.')
- o Don't label or diagnose. ('You're neurotic.' 'You're paranoid.')
- o Don't over-interpret. (Assuming a relationship is over because of one disagreement or by blaming someone's upbringing on the way they behave today.)
- o Don't distract or be irrelevant. ('Let's go somewhere else.' 'Do we have to talk about this? Why don't we go out instead?')
- o Don't pretend to be attentive. ('Oh, that's so interesting.' Once you have lied you will not be believed the next time and it is unkind to the speaker.)
- o Don't place time pressures – it is off-putting to tell someone they'd better be quick.
- o Don't fiddle with things or tap your foot as these might be interpreted as feelings of irritation or impatience.
- o Don't break confidences – the speaker will not go to you again.

SESSION 15

Self-Confidence and Shyness

Task I (group discussion)

What is self-confidence?

Task 2 (individually or in pairs)

- Where have you got messages from about yourself?
- What are they?
- Are they true?
- How do you see yourself?
- How would you like yourself to be? (These should be realistic goals to aim for, not impossibilities.)

Shyness

To have the courage to go up to a stranger and start a conversation, you need to feel confident about not having your advances rejected. The following thoughts might help:

People go to social gatherings knowing they will be expected to talk – so unless they are rude to everyone the chances are they will talk back.

Even if you feel you do not have anything interesting to say, concentrate on the fact that the other person has. Be genuinely interested in them.

Remind yourself that people are very interesting creatures and that the more people you meet, the more you understand about them.

Task 3 (individually or in pairs)

Think of your personal social rules. Make a list of those that are unrealistic. (For example, a woman must never start a conversation with a man without first being introduced; believing you must be liked and approved of by everyone you meet; believing you must never make a mistake in social situations.) Where have these rules/ideas come from? Rewrite the rules to make them more sensible or realistic.

Task 4 (individually or in pairs)

1. Identify any negative thoughts you have that lead to shyness and social difficulties (e.g., I'm not very interesting to talk to and never know what to say when I meet people. I often stammer and always blush.) Think of positive alternative thoughts and write them down.

2. Pinpoint any social situation that you find stressful (e.g., going to a party or to an interview or to a formal meal with people from work.)

Then write at least three positive statements for you to remind yourself of, to help you cope with the situation when it happens again for:

(a) before the situation

(b) during the situation

(c) after the situation.

Use at Home

Improving self-esteem

Self-esteem (how you feel about yourself) is linked to self-confidence. If you do not have a feeling of self-worth, it is almost impossible to feel confident about yourself when you meet other people. How could you imagine anyone would want to talk to you if you think very little of yourself?

Task A: To improve your self-esteem

- Write a list of everything you can do.
- Write a list of everything you are good at.
- Recall every nice thing that has ever been said about you – whether at school, work, leisure, or from a stranger whose shopping you helped pick up.
- Recall every successful social function you have attended (parties, discos, dinners, dates, school trips).
- Recall how you felt when social events went well. (Warm, pleased, chuffed, happy, confident, excited, amusing, fun-to-be-with.)

Task B

Write down some bad things that people have said to you or about you that you know are true. Include in your list any reasons for a of lack of social success at any time. Now pick out parts of your character that you know you can change if you tried. (Leave the harder things until later.) Then write down what steps to take for each one to change the negative comments into positive ones.

Example: 'You always look miserable.'

Task B continued

Your goal is to mostly look happy. (It is unrealistic to always look happy.) Choose when it is important to look happy:

- When you meet someone to show that you are pleased to see them.
- When you get good news or you hear of someone else's good news.
- When you pass people in the street or at the shops – brighten their day with a smile (unless you live in an area where it is dangerous to do so; however, there will be some environments where this behaviour would be appropriate and safe such as in your work place or at a local club.)

Once you have worked on the smaller problems, tackle bigger ones using small steps. (You cannot change overnight – aim for a slow but permanent improvement.) Remember any changes that you make about yourself – are for yourself. Only change what you want changed.

INFORMATION SHEET

Self-confidence

Task 1 What is self-confidence?

Self-confidence is feeling good about yourself, regardless of what others do or say or what they have achieved. Any goal (life aim) is concentrated on what you want for yourself rather than trying to compete with others so you fulfil your own special needs, not other people's.

Understand your strengths and weaknesses and know you have the ability to change certain aspects of yourself if you wish. Depend on yourself to achieve your goals, not on luck or other people. (Although it is natural to want encouragement and support from others while doing something challenging.)

Any success must be measured against yourself (a before-and-after comparison), not against others who have entirely different qualities and characteristics to you. For example, for someone who has been wheelchair-bound for years, managing to stand up is a huge achievement (as it is for a baby, learning to walk) – yet to the physically able this would be considered an everyday occurrence. See yourself as you are now in the context of your own life and experiences.

Sometimes we have a child's view of perfection, believing we must be perfect in our body, our actions, our words and our decisions in all of our activities. Also, we determine what we mean by perfection by listening to others or by seeing what others achieve, setting ourselves impossible goals so that we are never satisfied with who we are.

It is better to determine our self-image from within, without looking for approval from others. It is healthier to please yourself than trying to live up to other people's unrealistic expectations. We are too easily swayed by negative comments from other people and we concentrate only on the worst.

True self-confidence is an inner acceptance, understanding and support of our true selves and shows itself in our ability to interact positively with others (i.e., experience social successes, however small). (A social success may be considered anything from someone returning a smile to having an active social network where you have the most connections.)

Task 2 Where have you got messages from about yourself?

From our parents and every one else we interact with.

Shyness

Task 3 of this session is based on information obtained from pages 153–154 of *Human Relationship Skills* by Professor Richard Nelson-Jones (1990) reproduced with the permission of Cassell plc, Wellington House, 125 Strand, London, England.

Task 3

- ○ *A woman must never start a conversation with a man without first being introduced.*
- ○ If I am not over-friendly my motives are not likely to be misinterpreted when I speak to someone of the opposite sex.

- ○ *I must be liked and approved of by everyone I meet.*
- ○ I might prefer to be liked but it is unreasonable to expect it from everyone. I still have friends even if just a few people like me.

- ○ *I must never make a mistake in social situations.*
- ○ If I make mistakes I can learn by them. To make mistakes is human.

- ○ *I must never reveal anything about myself that might be seen as negative.*
- ○ Nobody's perfect. If I am to have an honest and open relationship I need to reveal my vulnerabilities as well as my strengths.

Task 4

Negative thoughts you have that lead to shyness and social difficulties:

I'm not very interesting to talk to and never know what to say when I meet people. I often stammer and always blush. Other people probably have more interesting things to say than I. If I concentrate on asking them about their lives I shall learn more about other people and they will like the fact that I have shown genuine interest. Listening can be just as important as talking. Once I have got to know the other person a little, I will feel more relaxed and so be able to talk about myself in return.

Positive thoughts for stressful social situations:

1. Before the situation

- I look my best.
- I am calm now so there's no reason to feel anxious later.
- I do like people and this will give me a chance to meet others.
- I am lonely and the only way to get over it is to mix with other people.
- I might meet someone I really like.
- My future best friend might be there.
- It will give me something to talk about at work on Monday.

2. During the situation

- I don't have to be liked by everyone. I can do my best to be liked by one or two people.
- I'll concentrate on what other people have to say to get my mind off my shyness.
- I'll be ready with a smile if someone catches my eye.
- I'll compliment the host/ess on such a delightful party.
- This interview is good practice for the next one.
- This interview is giving me practice at performing under pressure.

3. After the situation

- The next time will be easier.
- I'm glad I went and did not shy away from my own fears and inadequacies.
- Once I'd got talking I began to enjoy myself.
- This has given me an opportunity to invite people to my place.
- I know what I did wrong and so shouldn't do it again.

Making Conversation

Talking to strangers

When you talk to people you don't know well or don't know at all, the type of things you say should be light and uninvolved. For example, it is not usual tell a complete stranger that you are upset because your parents are divorcing. It would make them feel uncomfortable.

Task 1 (in groups)

How would you start a conversation with a stranger?

What would you talk about?

How would you keep the conversation going?

How would you look?

How would you sit or stand?

How would you end a conversation?

Task 2 (in groups)

Two students are needed to role play. One student must make conversation and be responsible for starting the conversation, trying to keep it going and then ending the conversation. The other student is a stranger.

Setting 1

Two people stand next to one another on a station platform. The train is late.

Setting 2

Two people meet at a party.

Setting 3

Two people are standing in a queue in a shop.

Then discuss each role play. What made the conversation go well or badly? How did the other person behave? Was it easy to get him to talk?

Talking to people you know

Task 3 (in groups)

- How do you greet someone you know well?
- What do you talk about?
- How do you make sure the conversation is balanced, in other words, both of you taking turns to talk?

Making conversation

Task 1

How would you start a conversation with a stranger?

- Smile and say hello.
- Be loud enough to be heard.
- Talk about something that involves both of you because of where you are, for example, you both go to the same evening class – ask the other person what they think about the teacher or the course.
- Stick to general comments that anyone can listen to – do not make it private and secret.

What would you talk about?

- The weather.
- About being late.
- Something you have in common with the other person such as being in the same place, for example, 'What a wonderful view' or 'The last time I travelled by train I was delayed by an hour because …'
- If you genuinely find something about the other person that you admire, tell them so – it is likely to make them warm to you (chat-up lines are usually insincere – this is not what we are talking about).
- You could talk about something that has been in the news recently such as an environmental disaster and ask them their opinion on the matter.
- You could mention something that might interest the other person, for example: 'I can recommend the film… I saw it last week.'

How would you keep the conversation going?

- Make sure your voice is loud and clear enough to be heard.
- Remember some general things to say that you can use anywhere.
- Pick up on any replies you get and ask more about what was said or comment on your view of what was said.
- Search for things you have in common so that the conversation is more likely to flow. (It should not be a series of questions fired at the other person.)

How would you look?

- o Look the other person in the eye.

- o Look confident and smile. Nod in agreement when appropriate.

How would you sit or stand?

- o Face the person you wish to speak to. Lean towards the other person.

How would you end a conversation?

- o There may be a natural break, for example, if your bus arrives and the other person is waiting for a different bus.

- o Say, 'Goodbye', or 'Nice to have met you', or 'Perhaps we'll bump into each other again sometime.' If appropriate say, 'Good luck with…'

- o Step back and turn your body away so the other person knows you are ready to leave.

Task 3

How do you greet someone you know well? Greet the person warmly with a big smile. Look genuinely pleased to see them. Popular people tend to reward the people they talk to in this way.

What do you talk about? Ask about the other person's health and life. Ask about things that are important to the other person. Tell the other person about good things that have happened to you. (Save the bad things for a best friend unless you simply state a fact – don't put off the other person with an unexpectedly heavy conversation.)

How do you make sure the conversation is balanced – in other words, both of you taking turns to talk? Listen to what the other person has to say. Make appropriate responses ('Uh-ha', nods, 'Oh dear…') Watch the other person when you speak – does she look bored? Is she yawning? This is known as social feedback and is very important in letting you know how you are doing.

Making conversation with people you know

The following are only suggestions. How you use them will depend on the individual and the circumstances. For example, if you always have trouble remembering names when you're 'on the spot', nudge your memory while you have plenty of time to think.

Unexpected meeting

1. Say, 'Hello' and smile to show you are really pleased to meet the person.
2. Talk about when you last saw one another.
3. Say something positive about any changes such as a haircut, a smart suit, how well they look.
4. Ask the person how they are.
5. Ask how their job is going or how they are spending their time.
6. Recall your last conversation for ideas on openers – were they starting something new at the time? Was their mother ill? Use the information to show you have remembered and that you care about them.

When you might meet someone, so have had some warning

1. Say, 'Hello' and smile widely to show you are really pleased to meet the person.
2. If you are likely to bump into someone you know (e.g., shopping in a small village, catching a regular train), remind yourself of the people you might meet such as, their and their partner's name, children's names, place of work or study, job/subject details so that you won't be stuck for something to say.
3. If there is something you always have trouble recalling, bring it to mind before you are likely to meet so that you won't struggle for the memory later.

Planned meeting

1. Say, 'Hello' and smile widely to show you are really pleased to meet the person.

2. Think of all the things mentioned above plus remind yourself of other details – where the person lives and who with, what their ambitions are, any particular event they have aimed for (such as a competition or an interview for a new job), whether they've recently celebrated a birthday or any other event such as parents retiring or attended a funeral or wedding.

3. Remember your last conversation and think of a couple of points to ask about to link your last meeting with this one, allowing you to pick up where you left off.

4. Have some ideas on what you would like to say about yourself – if you do not know the person well, think of mainly positive things to say to keep the conversation light.

5. Do not burden an unsuspecting person with all your worries. Be prepared to give away some things – saying everything is 'fine' does not allow the conversation to flow because then the person you meet has to think of another question to avoid awkward silences.

6. As a safety measure think up general topics that you would be able to comfortably discuss, without causing an argument, between either of you.

7. If you and this other person have friends in common (form part of the same network) remind yourself of any confidences you must keep – either information about another person or anything you have heard about the person you are going to meet. (Good news such as them getting a job is usually common knowledge and then you are free to openly congratulate them unless the original hearer was told to keep quiet about it.) If the person you meet tells you something you already know but you had to keep quiet about knowing, pretend their telling you is the first time you heard the news.

Conclusion

Social essentials

1. Respect the other person's privacy.
2. Make eye contact during conversation.
3. Do not discuss what has been told to you in confidence with others.
4. Do not criticise the other person publicly.
5. Be rewarding.
6. To become intimate deeper levels of self-disclosure are necessary.
7. Overcome negative thoughts about yourself and turn them into positive ones.

Qualities needed for being a good friend

- Showing warmth, sympathy, kindness, gentleness, cheerfulness.
- Being supportive in times of need.
- Sharing confidences and trust.
- Having non-judgemental attitudes towards others.
- Having positive attitudes towards friendship – so you are accepted and liked.

Part 3

Introduction

The introduction is based on information obtained from pages 273–274 of *Social Skills in Interpersonal Communication* by Owen Hargie, Christine Saunders and David Dickson (1994) published by Routledge and reproduced with permission.

In addition to the development of social skills, assertiveness skills are essential to command respect without the detrimental use of aggression or the put-down of self attitude of submission. Assertiveness skills aid better communication and assist in dealing with conflict at work, protect against racial, sexist and more general put-downs and allow clear criticism to be administered without the burden of emotional loading that can detract from the original aim. Assertiveness also aids the graceful acceptance of compliments and the complimenting of others in a more meaningful way.

Assertiveness skills help individuals to:

1. ensure their personal rights are not violated
2. withstand unreasonable requests from others
3. make reasonable requests of others
4. deal effectively with unreasonable refusals from others
5. recognise the personal rights of others
6. change the behaviour of others towards them
7. avoid unnecessary aggressive conflicts
8. confidently and openly communicate their position on any issue

Counselling skills are important in a relationship (at work or within a social network) where the other person faces a dilemma and can see no way through. Counselling involves helping the other person to look at their problem more objectively and to find their own solution. This is a more valuable experience than passing the responsibility of decision-making over to an adviser and later accusing this third party of making a bad judgement. Or, the other person, having missed the opportunity of helping themselves through sympathetic support alone, failed to increase their own self-esteem.

Assertiveness

Aggressive behaviour punishes (e.g., putting someone down, calling someone lazy or any other non-pleasing name) or threatens ('If you don't do this I'll...'). Aggressive people shout and give uncomfortable body messages (e.g., hands on hips, leaning over someone, scowling).

Unassertive behaviour is timid behaviour (e.g., saying sorry all the time even when it is not your fault, not standing up for yourself or being forced into doing something you don't want to).

Assertive behaviour is positive – you explain your needs and feelings clearly without putting someone else down and showing respect for the other person. Any criticism you give is useful (e.g., 'You might find it easier if you do it this way...').

Assertive people respect other people's values, experiences, background and religion. They can also choose whether or not they wish to be assertive, depending on the circumstances.

Assertive people stand up for themselves; can say, 'No' to people when necessary; can express their feelings and needs; can actively try to change their life when necessary (rather than unrealistically waiting for things to happen, like a job falling into their lap). Assertive people can protect themselves from put-downs and can deal well with disagreements.

Task 1 (in groups)

Say whether these people are aggressive, assertive or unassertive and give reasons why.

1. Jane makes her own clothes. One of her flatmates keeps asking her to sew her buttons back on when they fall off and to hem her skirt when it comes undone. Jane often says she's too busy to do it but her flatmate badgers her until Jane gives in. Jane feels resentful that her flatmate can't even be bothered to take the right colour of cotton round for her to use so that she has to use her own or buy it.

2. Heidi's employer asked her to stay behind after work to help finish a project, but Heidi had bought theatre tickets for that night and did not have the time to spare. She told her employer that she could not stay on that night but would be happy to work overtime the following night if that was any good.

3. John kept turning up for work late and when his boss asked him whether he had such a thing as an alarm clock, John replied it was none of his damned business.

4. Nikolai was teased about his accent by his classmates. He decided he couldn't stand another day of it so told them firmly that he'd had enough of them and that he was going to tell the headmaster about it.

Task 2 (in groups)

For the following situations say something assertive.

1. You are in a supermarket queue and someone pushes in front of you.

2. Your work mate has taken credit from your boss for something you did.

3. You don't understand why you got such a low grade for your last assignment. You thought it was brilliant.

4. You are told off for being late yet again when it was only your first time.

5. You find out that your work mate who started after you and does the same job earns more money than you.

6. You have always agreed to work late whenever your boss has asked you to, but this evening you've arranged to out with some friends and your boss has asked you to work late again.

Task 3 (in groups)

Think of an occasion when you have behaved aggressively towards someone. What happened? Who said what? Who did what? What could you have said or done to behave assertively at that time?

Think of an occasion when you have behaved passively towards someone. What happened? Who said what? Who did what? What could you have said or done to behave assertively at that time?

Assertiveness

Task 1

Say whether these people are aggressive, assertive or unassertive and give reasons why.

1. Jane is unassertive because she does not stand up for what she wants. She cannot say 'No' to her flatmate and stick to it. She is rewarding her flatmate for badgering her by showing that she always gives in. Jane does not express her feelings about the way she is being used nor does she set her 'guidelines', for example, 'I'll sew that for you as long as you provide the thread'.

2. Heidi is assertive because she shows that she cannot change her plans once made but is willing to help out at another time. (She could choose to change her plans if it was convenient for her – this does not show a lack of assertion, but if she had changed her plans against her will she would have felt resentful and then she would have behaved passively, like Jane above.)

3. John is aggressive. It was reasonable to expect his boss to question him about being late even though his boss had behaved aggressively by using sarcasm. John was not respecting the rights of his boss and should not have been rude. He was in the wrong so should have apologised about his lateness.

4. Nikolai is assertive because he recognised he had the right not to be treated like that and decided to do something about it. Bullying is aggressive behaviour and Nikolai responded to that openly by telling the others he would not accept it anymore.

Task 2

In the following situations say what you could say to be assertive.

1. Excuse me, you might not have noticed, but you've just taken my place.

2. Why did you let Mrs X think you did it when you knew it was my work? I want you to tell her the truth the next time you see her.

   Or: Why did you let Mrs X think you did it when you knew it was my work? What are you going to do about it?

3. Would you mind explaining how I got this grade? You see, I spent so much time on this piece that I felt sure it was worth a higher grade.

4. I'm very sorry I was late, my bus was delayed. Why do you think I've been late before? This was my first time.

5. May I have a word? I feel upset because I heard that Robert's salary is higher than mine – not because I'm jealous but because I feel undervalued. I thought our jobs were exactly the same.

6. No, not tonight, I've already made plans.

Protecting Yourself

A put-down is a voice or body message that is meant to make you feel small or bad about yourself (and it is a type of bullying).

The more often we challenge a put-down, the less often it will happen as people will know they can not get away with such behaviour.

Put-downs are sometimes partly true. Accept the part that is true and reject the part that is not.

Sometimes, it is just an expression that someone makes that implies something about you like raised eyebrows may mean they do not believe you – so say, 'I don't understand why you raised your eyebrows. What were you trying to say?'

Whether it is a voice or body message, ask for things to be made clearer so that you understand what the other person means. For example, 'Are you implying I'm stupid? Why do you think that? Give me an example.' Then either agree or disagree with them over that one instance.

If the person cannot think of any examples, tell them to let you know the next time you do something they dislike so that you can talk about it. You must be given the chance to explain your side or to defend yourself.

Example: Dealing with a put-down

Attack: Your boss must be very patient with his employees.

Defence: What do you mean?

Attack: Well, because you don't pick up things quickly.

Defence: Pick up what?

Attack: New skills. You mentioned how long it took you to learn how to use the photocopier.

Defence: Are you implying I'm stupid?

Attack: Well, slow.

Defence: It did take me a while to get to grips with the upgraded photocopier. Since the old one was very basic there were a lot of functions on the new one I hadn't used before. I like to be thorough so that I get things right. Once I've learnt a new task I'm not slow. It is not fair to base your opinion of me on that one incident.

A statement of fact, for example, 'You're black', is not necessarily a put-down. However, 'You're one of those blacks', is a racial put-down. This statement is loaded with dislike and prejudice.

Put-downs can be against people of a different race, sex, physical ability, class, social standing, amount of wealth (or lack of wealth). They can be against anyone with anything that is different. Often people say nasty things about others because they are jealous of something and use the person's differences as a weapon.

Zak

Zak told his mum's neighbour the good news. His girlfriend had agreed to marry him. She stood open-mouthed. 'But you're disabled. You're in a wheelchair. People in wheelchairs can't, well, you know...' She felt confused. Why get married if they can't have sex or children?

Task 1 (in one large or several smaller groups)

The story about Zak shows one example of stereotyping. Is it true that all people in wheelchairs are unable to have a sexual relationship? What is stereotyping? Give some examples.

Natalie

Natalie saw two women walking down the street one Saturday night holding hands. She said to her friend, 'I can't stand lesbians.' Her friend replied, 'Do you know any?' Natalie said, 'No, but I know of them.'

Task 2 (in one large or several smaller groups)

The story about Natalie is one example of prejudical behaviour. Why did Natalie say she couldn't stand lesbians? How could she say that if she didn't know any? Even if she did know one lesbian and didn't like her, does that mean she wouldn't like all of them? What is prejudice? Give some examples.

People with low self-esteems often put themselves down. (This is belittling yourself.) This gives others signals that you will not stand up for yourself so they might be tempted to take advantage of you or bully you.

Task 3 (in one large or several smaller groups)

What put-downs have people aimed at you? What did you do about them? What assertive response could you have given?

Task 4 (in one large or several smaller groups)

Give assertive responses to the following put-downs:
1. 'You're one of those blacks.'
2. 'You're just like your mother.'
3. 'What do you want to go to a disco for when you're in a wheelchair?'
4. 'It's not ladylike to be a mechanic.'
5. 'Robert, you want to be a hairdresser? Isn't that a job for pansies?'
6. 'You? Get a job?'

Protecting Yourself

Prejudice is a preconceived opinion – either liking or disliking something. Prejudice is based on ignorance.

Examples:

- o 'I don't like foreigners.'
- o 'You're not going to that place.'
- o 'I'm not having a student as a tenant.'

Stereotyping is giving a fixed, exaggerated description about a certain group or society based on prejudice rather than fact. By repetition over time, stereotypes become fixed in people's minds, resistant to change even when there is evidence to the contrary.

Examples:

- o 'All women want babies.'
- o 'The Irish are stupid.'
- o 'Women's work is in the kitchen.'
- o 'Disabled people can't marry.'

For any stereotypical put-down, you can mention the fact that you are an individual and that judgement cannot be made on your lifestyle or behaviour based on someone's previous experience with others.

Assertive responses to the following put-downs:

1. 'You're one of those blacks.'

Response: 'What do you mean? Which other black people do you know and why are you grouping me with them? I don't group you with the whites I know. I understand you're an individual.'

2. 'You're just like your mother.'

Response: 'In what way am I like her? I can't be exactly like her.'

3. 'What do you want to go to a disco for when you're in a wheelchair?'

Response: 'I enjoy socialising with the rest of my friends. I like to see them dance and I enjoy listening to the music. Discos are very lively places.'

4. 'It's not ladylike to be a mechanic.'

Response: 'That's an old-fashioned view. There are plenty of jobs women do now that were traditionally only done by men and it doesn't make them any less feminine. If you take being ladylike to such an extreme, then women shouldn't go out to work at all. Most women need to work and we have a right to choose what we are interested in and good at.'

5. 'Robert, you want to be a hairdresser? Isn't that a job for pansies?'

Response: 'Being in a creative job doesn't make me any more or less masculine. Besides, I think I would be really good at it.'

6. 'You? Get a job?'

Response: 'Why do you say that? Why shouldn't I get a job?'

Feelings and Complaints

Expressing your feelings

Start your sentence with 'I...' or 'My...' and say how you feel about a situation. Don't begin a sentence with 'You...' as it is likely to put the person's back up (it may be seen by them as aggressive – putting all the blame onto them.)

Example

When you are angry say, 'I feel angry because you haven't listened to what I've said.' Not, 'You make me sick!' Be very clear about what you want to say, telling the other person how it has affected you. For example, 'I'm unhappy because my dog died', instead of saying: 'Leave me alone.' 'I feel hurt when you ignore me', instead of saying: 'Don't turn away from me!' 'My view is different to yours. When...', instead of saying: 'You're wrong.'

Task 1 (in groups)

Give assertive, 'feeling' responses to the following situations:
1. Your partner's late yet again when meeting you/picking you up.
2. Your friend tells someone else your secrets.

Making a complaint

Consider:

- what happened (promise broken over sharing of housework)
- with whom it happened (my friend)

- when it happened (the weekend)
- how often it has happened before (two other times)
- what you want done about it (promise to be kept and ironing done)
- what terms are you going to set? (refuse to share housework unless the ironing is done tonight)

Make your boundaries clear. You must be prepared to carry out any terms you set or you will not be taken seriously.

Response: You promised me that if I cooked on the weekend you'd do all the ironing. This is the third time you haven't done what you'd said. I'm not going to cook for you anymore unless you finish the ironing tonight.

Task 2 (in groups)

Write assertive responses to the following situations:

1. Your flatmate does jobs badly so that she won't be asked to do them again. Today she cleaned the bathroom while you shopped. There were scale marks round the bath and hairs in the plug hole.

2. The person who brings the post to your desk each morning brings it late and your boss expects you to have dealt with it much earlier.

Dealing with complaints

Stay calm. If you are called names, ignore them or make a short comment about them without name-calling back. Accept any fault that is your own and apologise. If you work for a company which is responsible, be ready to act as a go-between. Explain it is not your fault but the company's and you will try to sort out the problem.

Example

You work behind the till in a bank and the queue is very long. Your next customer is very angry and says, 'It's disgraceful the way we are expected to wait. You should employ more people. Banks make enough money out of us!'

Response: I'm sorry you've had to wait so long. We do employ more staff but three are off sick with 'flu. I'm working as quickly as I can but I do have to make sure all transactions are accurate. I realise your time is precious and I won't keep you any longer than necessary.

Example

You take telephone calls for holiday bookings. A customer has just arrived back from a disastrous holiday and is taking his anger out on you. He says, 'You must have known the hotel was next to a building site, but you still took my money you bastards!'

Response: There is no need to swear at me. I am sorry your holiday did not go well. May I suggest you write us a letter detailing your complaints so that we can look into the matter.

Task 3 (in groups)

Write assertive responses to the following situations:

1. You are a waitress and you have got someone's order wrong. They are angry with you and demand to see the manager. It is your first day at work.

2. Your parents tell you that you are selfish as you never help out in the home. They say it's about time you pulled your weight and did your share.

Dealing with conflict

In an argument or disagreement, keep calm. Don't put the blame on the other person but try to mend whatever damage has been done. Don't try to 'win' – if the other person has the same attitude there is little chance of sorting out the problem. Talk about what you agree on and then discuss the things you don't agree on and try to find a middle ground (compromise) that can suit you both.

Example

At work, the office cannot be left empty during office hours. The boss always goes out for a long lunch. Your colleague has lunch first but is often late back, which means you get your lunch late and you have less time.

You:　　I'd like to swap the lunch breaks so that I go out first. You nearly always come back late and it's not fair on me.

Colleague: No. This is how it was agreed when I started here.

You:　　Well, how about having a rota? You could then go out first every other day – every fortnight we'd each have had the same number of lunch-times first.

Task 4 (in groups)

Suggest a fair compromise for each of the following situations:

1.　You share a kitchen with three others. You always find dirty saucepans in the sink that the others haven't bothered to wash up. So when you want to cook, you have to wash up one of their saucepans first. (All kitchen materials are shared.)

2.　Your parents keep getting angry with you for coming home late because they are worried about you. Also, because they can't go to sleep until you're in they are getting tired and grumpy.

Feelings and Complaints

Task 1

1. *Your partner's late yet again when picking you up.*

   Response: I feel you don't respect me when you don't turn up on time. If you can't come when we arranged, why don't you 'phone or say beforehand that it's too early? I feel belittled and upset when I'm kept waiting time and again.

2. *Your friend tells someone else your secrets.*

   Response: I feel betrayed by you. What I told you was in confidence, yet you didn't keep it to yourself.

Task 2

1. *The friend you share a flat with seems to deliberately do any job badly so that she won't be asked to do it again. Today she cleaned the bathroom while you shopped. There were scale marks round the bath and hairs in the plug hole.*

   Response: We agreed to share the housework. It's no good having marks around the bath and the plug hole full of hair. Unless you do your jobs properly from now on, I think it would be better if we looked after ourselves separately. If you still don't clean up after yourself, I'll look for somewhere else to live and you'll have to find someone else to share the rent with.

2. *The person who brings the post to your desk each morning brings it late and your boss expects you to have dealt with it much earlier.*

   Response: I don't get the post until nearly ten o'clock – yet it's delivered to the building by nine. I need to have the post on my desk earlier so that I can deal with it before my boss gets in. If you don't get it to me promptly, I'll have to complain to personnel.

Task 3

1. *You are a waitress and you have got someone's order wrong. They are angry with you and demand to see the manager. It is your first day at work.*

Response: I am very sorry about your order, it was an unfortunate mistake. I wish you'd let me change the meal for you. It's my first day at work and I am still learning. I might lose my job if you complain to the manager.

2. *Your parents tell you that you are selfish as you never help out in the home. They say it's about time you pulled your weight and did your share.*

    Response: You're right I could do more. At the moment I'm studying for my final exam. Could we sort out what you want me to do when the exam's over?

Task 4

1. *You share a kitchen with three others. You always find dirty saucepans in the sink that the others haven't bothered to wash up. So when you want to cook, you have to wash up one of their saucepans first. (All kitchen materials are shared.)*

    Response: Could we have a rule that we wash up as soon as we've finished eating what we cooked? It's not fair that I have to clean up after someone else before I can get my own meal sorted.

    Or: I've bought my own pans so that I don't have to wash up after you before I can cook something myself. Please don't use them.

2. *Your parents keep getting angry with you for coming home late because they are worried about you. Also, because they can't go to sleep until you're in they are getting tired and grumpy.*

    Response: Can I have friends back to the house Saturday nights so you'll have me home earlier? If there's something special on like a party I could ring to say I'm all right before you go to bed and wake you up when I get in.

Saying No, Compliments and Asking for What You Want

Saying 'no'

When someone has asked you to do something you really don't want to, you should say, 'No'. Often words alone are not enough. You have to look and sound as though you mean, 'No'. Have a serious expression that shows no doubt or hesitation. Firmly and clearly say, 'No'. If you think the situation demands it, give a reason.

People who are unable to say, 'No' are taken advantage of. This lowers self-respect and self-esteem.

Task 1 (in groups)

Give an assertive refusal for the following situations (more than just a 'No' so that you think more deeply about expressing yourself.)

1. Your workmate is often late but expects you to cover for him by saying he's just popped out to the loo or has gone to a different department. If you get caught lying it will ruin your reputation of being a responsible employee.

2. A friend invites you out but you can't stand her boyfriend and he always tags along.

Giving compliments

For a compliment to be meaningful, it needs to be specific, not vague. If you like something, say why you like it. If you want to praise someone, be generous and say why they deserve it. And don't give compliments by putting yourself down as it belittles what you are saying. (For example, 'You're so clever. I could never do that.')

Example

A friend has just passed his driving test.

> *Response:* That's wonderful news. I'm so glad, well done.(*Not:* That's great. I don't think I'll ever pass mine.)

Task 2 (in groups)

Give meaningful compliments for the following situations:

1. A friend arrives at a fancy dress party, her clothes and her hair look completely different. You didn't recognise her and the outfit is stunning.

2. A neighbour's garden is full of bright, colourful flowers. You stop to admire it and see her weeding by the gate.

Receiving compliments

Accept compliments gracefully. If someone admires what you are wearing don't say, 'This? I've had it for years.' Instead say, 'Thank you for noticing. I wasn't sure whether it suited me or not.'

This rewards the person who gave you the compliment and encourages them to compliment you again in the future. If you ignore a compliment or brush it off they are less likely to say something nice in the future.

Task 3 (in groups)

Give responses to accept these compliments gracefully:

1. Your keyboard skills are excellent.

2. I admire you for coping so well at home, looking after your mother and younger brother and sister. It can't be easy.

Asking for what you want

If you want something changed or done, you should explain your needs clearly without making demands.

You should tell people what your needs are as they cannot be expected to guess them. But remember that the other person has the right to say, 'No'.

Example

You need more time for an assignment as you are a bridesmaid/page boy/best man at a wedding this weekend.

Response: May I have an extra three days to finish my work? I'm going to be a bridesmaid at a wedding this weekend.

Task 4 (in groups)

Give assertive requests for the following situations:

1. You need more space (time to yourself) as a friend is crowding you. You want to be able to see other friends as well.

2. Your friend speaks very loudly, broadcasting your conversation wherever you are.

Saying No, Giving Compliments and Asking for What you Want

Task 1

1. *Your work mate is often late but expects you to cover for him by saying he's just popped out to the loo or has gone to a different department. If you get caught lying it will ruin your reputation of being a responsible employee.*

    Response: I'm not covering up for you again. I'm not prepared to take the risk of being caught out with a lie and it's unfair of you to ask me.

2. *A friend invites you out but you can't stand her boyfriend and he always tags along.*

    Response: I don't want to. I prefer seeing you on your own. Can't we go out sometime together or with just the girls?

Task 2

1. *A friend arrives at a fancy dress party and is transformed by her clothes and hair style. You didn't recognise her and the outfit is stunning.*

    Response: You've dressed up so cleverly, I didn't recognise you until you spoke to me. The clothes really suit you and you look stunning.

2. *A neighbour's garden is full of bright, colourful flowers. You stop to admire it and see her weeding by the gate.*

    Response: Your garden is fabulous. I've never seen so many beautiful flowers in one place. You've done a wonderful job.

Task 3

1. *Your keyboard skills are excellent.*

    Response: Thank you. I've practised a lot. I'm glad you noticed.

2. *I admire you for coping so well at home, looking after your mother and younger brother and sister. It can't be easy.*

    Response: It is hard but I feel quite proud that I've managed. It's given me a lot of confidence.

Task 4

1. *You need more space (time to yourself) as a friend is crowding you. You want to be able to see other friends as well.*

    Response: I need to spend some time alone as I feel I never have a moment to myself or to spend time with other friends. Could we see each other every other weekend instead of every week?

2. *Your friend speaks very loudly, broadcasting your conversation wherever you are.*

    Response: Could you talk more softly so that other people won't be able to hear?

My Rights

1.   I have the right to express my feelings and opinions.

2.   I have the right to say 'No'.

3.   I have the right to make mistakes and cope with the consequences.

4.   I have the right to change my mind.

5.   I have the right to success.

6.   I have the right to ask for what I want.

7.   I have the right to be treated with respect.

8.   I have the right to refuse responsibility for other people's problems.

Remember that everyone else has these rights too!

Concluding Assertiveness

1. Do not 'put-down' another person – this is a verbal form of bullying.

2. Do not become aggressive (threatening behaviour, shouting, swearing).

3. Do not over-apologise – it becomes embarrassing to the other person and the apologiser loses self-respect.

4. Do not seek revenge. This is an aggressive response.

5. Do not manipulate people – this is dishonest communication, pretending to be something you are not.

6. Avoid conflict by finding common ground and negotiating from that point of agreement.

7. Avoid 'I must win' arguments.

8. Be specific when complaining and stick to the point. Avoid anger and abuse.

9. You can choose when to be angry and when to avoid conflict.

10. Accept compliments with grace and give meaningful compliments.

Counselling

Introduction

Counselling is helping someone to look at their problems so that they can find their own solutions. It helps them to have a clear picture of their problem in their minds and to unravel confusing ideas.

Counselling is not solving the problem for someone else but helping them find their own, most appropriate, solution and acting on it themselves with the emotional support of the counsellor.

Counselling is not giving advice – if it were, too much responsibility and control would be in the hands of the counsellor, depriving the person of developing their own way of coping with the problem or having the satisfaction of being able to find and carry out their own solutions.

Accepting advice discourages independence and puts blame on the advisor when things go wrong. People should accept responsibility for their own actions and inactions.

It is far better to discover what to do through talking about problems and thinking more deeply about the situation. In other words, to go on a journey of self-discovery, accompanied by a sympathetic companion giving support and encouragement along the way until the person is sufficiently confident to go it alone.

We can use counselling skills to communicate sincerely and sensitively with other people in a variety of relationships, settings and situations, encouraging trust and honesty with which to build good relationships. The experience of counselling helps us to make our own decisions and take responsibility for our own lives.

Task 1 (in one large group): put ideas on the chalkboard or overhead projector

Discuss the following:

- What is counselling about?
- What would you expect a counsellor to be like?
- What qualities do you think a counsellor needs? (Think about when you have listened to a friend or sibling in need.)
- Why is counselling important?
- Why do people need counselling?
- What could happen if someone needed help and there was no one to discuss the problem with?
- What help is available outside school/college/work?
- Would you go to someone for help if you felt you needed it?
- Who would you choose and why?
- What situations do you think require counselling? (You might suggest reasons from your own experiences.)

Task 2: Preparation for Session 22 (allow about 15 minutes in total)

You need to decide on something that worries you (for whatever reason) and write it in one sentence on a piece of paper. The gathering of this information will be anonymous as the pieces of paper will be collected in a box. The problems will be used for role play in the next few sessions.

Task 3 (in one large group)

Read 'The Essentials of Counselling' sheets and discuss their meaning. This will help you understand what counselling is about.

Counselling

Task I

Discuss what counselling is about. Counselling is helping people overcome distress from — relationship breakdowns, physical trauma (mugging, domestic violence), emotional trauma (bereavement), lack of confidence, anxiety, fear or phobia.

Counselling is assisting the individual to fulfil themselves by helping them discover the power and resources they already possess so that they gain control over their own lives. The individuals grow slowly to manage their own position in the present and the future.

What would you expect a counsellor to be like? Someone who is sympathetic and able to give time to listen to your problems in confidence in a non-judgemental way, enabling you to build up your own self-esteem rather than casting blame and criticising. A counsellor would not tell or advise on what to do, although they might ask your opinion on some suggestions if you have no ideas yourself.

What qualities are needed from a counsellor? Patience, ability to listen, wanting to help others, liking people, not being biased in any way, sensitivity, able to sit back from a situation and not get emotionally involved, good concentration, good memory, able to express themselves clearly, able to sum up situations, able to relate to others, able to empathise, able to refer to someone else if they are unable to help, able to be tactful, able to take a passive role — not telling a person how to run their lives, and so on.

Why is counselling important? Because it helps a distressed person to help themselves and become more effective as individuals. It increases the individual's ability to cope with a range of problems and so increases the control they have over their own lives and their self-esteem.

Why do people need it? Because many of us are damaged by life events and cannot cope with the feelings we have. If we want to improve our ability to cope with life we need help and understanding from others especially if we have difficulty in relating to people. Often we cannot find our own way through life and need help in discovering avenues to explore, with the appropriate coping techniques.

What could happen if someone needed help and there was no one to discuss the problem with? If the person is very desperate they might attempt or succeed in killing themselves or take out their anguish on others – including domestic violence, battering, abuse of different kinds or resorting to medication to dull their feelings.

What help is available outside school/college? Telephone help lines such as: Childline (sexual and physical abuse), SANELINE (any mental distress or illness), Samaritans (any problem, especially depression, loneliness, feelings of desperation, suicide), Rape Crisis (rape and sexual abuse), Cruse (bereavement). There are many forms of counselling available through voluntary and professional groups. Some counselling is available through referrals from doctors.

Essentials of Counselling

This sheet is based on information obtained from pages 73 and 74 of *Successful Interviewing in a Week* by Mo Shapiro, (1993) published by Institute of Management/ Hodder and Stoughton and reproduced with permission.

The person you want to help knows him/herself and what s/he wants better than anyone else, including you. You must let him/her change his/her own behaviour in a way that helps to solve his/her problem in the best possible way. You must accept that s/he has the ability and the means within him/herself to get what s/he wants – you must not try and do it for him/her.

Three essential counselling skills

BEING GENUINE

This means having a real interest in, and desire to help the person so that you trust and respect each other. In your mind give him/her the same importance as yourself so that you are seen as being equal. Respond easily to what is said and say helpful things so that s/he is encouraged to be open and honest back. Be yourself and don't put on an act of playing a professional.

VALUING A PERSON WITHOUT JUDGING

The person should be valued, whatever s/he has done or how s/he feels so that s/he can share feelings without fear of being made to feel bad. You must not be judgemental or assume his/her values and beliefs are the same as yours (e.g., religion/upbringing). S/he must be respected (but not necessarily his/her behaviour).

PUTTING YOURSELF IN THEIR SHOES

This is understanding his/her feelings and experiences, seeing life from his/her point of view. Ideally, both of you should give and receive warmth and genuineness.

CONFIDENTIALITY

You must not discuss what has been said with anyone else without his/her permission. However, it is often possible to get help without anyone knowing who it is you are troubled about. (You may need advice on how to handle a situation if you feel out of your depth or if you are so upset by what you have heard that you need to talk to someone about it.) But whatever you do: confidentiality must be assured. Don't treat him/her differently because of your extra knowledge and don't make excuses for his/her behaviour or cover up for him/her – it will become known that s/he has a problem. (And then you would have broken the pact of confidentiality.)

Essentials of counselling

RESPONSIBILITIES OF THE PERSON SEEKING HELP

S/he should recognise that s/he is in a situation s/he wants to either improve or change and show that s/he really wants to do something to make this happen. (S/he must not rely on the counsellor to do everything for him/her and then blame the counsellor when it goes wrong.)

S/he must always own his/her problems, the choices and the decisions s/he makes. They are not taken away or solved by the counsellor. Suggestions you make may be either accepted as possibilities or rejected – but the responsibility always lies with the person seeking help.

THE COUNSELLOR SHOULD

- Invite the person to talk but do not force him/her. S/he must be willing.
- If you cannot spare the time to counsel when a request is made, give an alternative time.
- Choose an area that will be quiet with no interruptions. And then give your full attention.

Preparation and Instructions for Session 22

Preparation

Write or type the students' problems gathered in Session 21 on a piece of paper, leaving sufficient space between each sentence so that they can be cut up and given out as individual problems. (If the students do not wish to use their own problems, make up some of your own or use the problems given in the Problem Bank on page 172, 177 or 179.)

The session: instructions

Seat the group either in two concentric rings with each student facing the other – or in rows where students face each other. Give each student sitting in the outer ring or rows a piece of paper with a problem on it. They then explain their problem to the person sitting opposite to them who must try and give some help within two to three minutes. After this time the outer ring and rows move across one seat (clockwise) and then explain their problem to the new person sitting opposite them. (The 'helpers' do not move.)

After a few seat changes, ask the students to swap problems in a clockwise direction and to continue moving round at the end of each two-minute stretch.

Next swap the helpers from the outer ring and rows to the inner ring (this can be done by passing problems to the people opposite after a seat change but before any help is given). (This approach has been called a 'carousel'.)

Purpose

As well as gathering ideas on how to help others, students will become aware of others' worries, be encouraged to divulge their own problems with trusted friends and will be provided with a discussion point on whether this was 'counselling'.

Conclusion

Discuss problems that were addressed in the 'carousel' and see if help given by students had points in common – did they all say the same thing or were the ideas very different? If there was a range of suggestions (even conflicting ones) discuss why this was so and if they can come up with a collective solution.

This may lead to discussion that in life there is often no one correct answer, that we all have slightly different (if not very different) views and experiences and values. Such is sometimes the danger of giving advice. What might be acceptable, for example, in one culture might be taboo in another.

Using the 'carousel', there is not the time for true counselling and there is too little information to act on. Because of this, students will inevitably make snapshot judgements, view the problem as an isolated worry without considering any deeper, underlying fears and try to solve the problem by giving advice.

Discuss the differences between counselling and the giving of advice. Both have their merits. Are there any particular circumstances that warrant giving quick advice? (For example, when a girl has unprotected sex and has no wish to conceive, the more promptly she acts, the easier it is to get help – e.g., the 'Morning After Pill' or the insertion of the IUD within days of intercourse. Here advice is valid – get to your doctor or your Family Planning Clinic.)

Examples of worries of teenagers collected in a school

1. I'm worried about not doing well in exams even though I work hard.

2. I'm worried about my family breaking up as my parents often argue.

3. I fancy my boyfriend but I don't know if he fancies me.

4. I'm worried about having spots and what to do about them.

5. I'm worried about there being a nuclear war and what will happen to us.

6. I'm worried about having to go to hospitals – they frighten me.

7. I'm worried about being too short.

8. I'm worried about being attacked or raped.

9. I'm worried about getting AIDS or fancying someone with AIDS.

10. I'm worried about not getting a job when I leave school.

11. I'm worried about someone close to me dying.

12. I'm worried about dying young or being ill a lot of my life.

13. I'm worried about not having a home to live in as my parents split up and I live with an aunt at the moment.

14. I'm worried about not having a home as we don't have very much money and often can't pay our bills.

15. I'm worried about not being able to get on with my parents.

16. I'm worried about getting a bad report.

17. I'm worried I won't always get my coursework finished on time.

18. I don't have many friends – I haven't got a best friend either.

19. I'm worried about getting involved with drugs and what would happen to me.

20. I don't enjoy school and I don't know what to do about it.

21. I don't think some teachers like me.

22. I'm worried my clothes aren't fashionable enough and that people will laugh at me.

23. I'm worried about the pain when I give birth to a baby when I'm older.

24. I'm worried I might get pregnant when I don't want to.

25. I'm scared of spiders – how can I overcome this?

Preparation and Instructions for Session 23

There are many instances in life when there isn't the opportunity or the time to give proper counselling – one is when answering a letter. But unbiased advice from a total outsider may give us useful insight into our problem that we may not have thought of ourselves – it is then up to us whether we follow any of the advice given in this way.

Preparation

Either collect teenage (or young adult) magazines for advice columns or ask students to bring some in themselves. (Boy and girl magazines.) Discuss the differences in the two types of magazine – which one concentrates more on advice in the problem pages. Why might this be? (Think back to the start of this course – girls' talk tends to be more intimate and problem-sharing based.)

In one large or several smaller groups, read out the problem and discuss the best way to reply. Then read out the response given in the magazine. Was their advice the same as that given by the agony aunt/uncle? If there was a difference, which was better? Why?

Ask girls to give advice on the boys' problems and boys to give advice on the girls' problems. Is this harder to do than for their own sex?

Are there general areas of problems with students in their age groups? What about for older teenagers or women/men – what problems do they have?

Some problems may need information to help students solve them or to put right myths or ideas that are dangerous or not sensible. Other problems might be impossible to solve, in which case it might be best to help the 'counselled' come to terms with the situation.

Counselling Skills

Remember some problems need specialist help and can't be dealt with by non-professionals.

Skills

Use correct body language

1. Show you are paying attention. (Face the person squarely, lean forward and make frequent eye contact.)

2. Sit without barriers between you (no desk or table) so that the individual's body language can be clearly seen and they will not feel distanced from you.

Listen actively

1. Track the person – check from time to time that you understand what is being said. Summarise what they've said to check your understanding of the situation or repeat back a sentence they have said (e.g., 'And then she hit you?') – this encourages the person to continue while letting them know they have your undivided attention.

2. Encourage the person with appropriate sounds (Umm. Yes. Oh?)

3. Listen out for subjects or areas that seem to be avoided.

Asking questions

1. Ask 'open' questions – ones that need more than a 'yes' or 'no' answer. ('Why was that?' or 'How did you feel?' instead of 'Was that because…?' or 'Did that make you angry?')

2. Repeat key words in the form of a question to encourage the other to open up without them feeling that they are being interrogated. ('Whenever she does that I feel small.' 'Small?')

3. Allow time for pauses and silences so that you both have time to think about what has been said and where you want to go next.

4. Use hypothetical questions so that the individual can explore options. ('What would happen if…?')

5. Find out what has changed so that you can compare the situation now with how it was, to give you both a greater understanding and to focus on where the difficulties are. ('How have things changed?' 'How did you feel about her before this happened?… How do you feel about her now?')

Developing rapport

Use the same words and speech patterns so that you do not emphasize the differences between you and the individual, as long as they would appear natural. (For example, if slang is used to describe something, use the same word.)

Sometimes it is useful to physically match the other person in terms of posture and gesticulations – but this must not be in an overt way or the person may think the counsellor is mimicking them which would make the situation worse.

Give necessary information

Do not say, 'This is what you need to know about… so you should realise that this is what you should do…' just say, 'Did you know that…?' If you do not know what the individual needs to know to help them come to a decision, tell them where to get it from, help them to find out or find it out for them.

Encourage thinking

Ask the person to look at different ways of tackling the problem and consider the consequences of various options. Make up a table of positive and negative attributes of each suggestion – with the individual supplying these thoughts.

Counselling in Practice[1]

As a group, discuss what the following three stages of counselling involve.

Stage 1: Understanding

This is a listening stage. It is all right to have silences.

- What is the person's story?
- How does s/he feel?
- Is there more than one problem?

Stage 2: Moving on

- Is there another way of looking at things?
- How have others managed?
- How many options are there?

Approaches

- Feedback – is there a reason for the problem?
- Probing – what would happen if you did that?
- Challenging – has s/he suggested a solution but not tried it out? If so, why not?
- Sharing your own experience – show you understand their problem but do not give details.

Stage 3: Action

- Goal setting.
- Provide on-going support.
- Review and evaluation.

1　This sheet is based on information obtained from pages 73 and 74 of *Successful Interviewing in a Week* by Mo Shapiro, (1993) published by Institute of Management/Hodder and Stoughton and reproduced with permission.

Approaches

- Goal setting – make sure the person's goal is clear, specific to their problem and attainable.
- Reviewing – check how progress is being made and change the goals if necessary.
- Referral – do not work outside your competence – refer to experts when necessary.

For the tasks, use problems from the Problem Bank (see p.172–186).

Task (in groups of three)

Students act as: (A) counsellor (B) counselled (C) observer

You will each be given a problem to solve. Think about how your problem would affect you and your home, college or work life – try to imagine you really have that difficulty – for about five minutes. Each of you will take turns to tell another about your problem.

Rotation I: IA, 2B, 3C

In each group, Student I counsels Student 2. Student 3 observes. (This should take about fifteen minutes.) (If you are unable to carry out your role play due to cultural or other reasons, please say so at the beginning so that you can be given an alternative situation.)

Feedback I

Student I (counsellor) now explains his or her answers to the following questions to the rest of the group:

- What is your understanding of the problem?
- What choices were talked about in order to change the situation?
- Were there problems with any of these choices?
- What do you think Student 2 (counselled student) wants to happen?
- How does s/he think it can be achieved?
- What is Student 2 going to do? (What goal was set?)

- How well did you feel the session went? (For example, was progress made?)

Now Student 2 (the counselled) describes to the rest of the group:

- How easy was it to talk about your problem?
- Did you feel encouraged by the counsellor to open up?
- Did you warm to the counsellor and want to tell him/her all your problems?
- How well do you think you explained your problem? (Did the counsellor understand the problem quickly and easily?)
- Did you feel that your problem was helped by the session?

Now Student 3 (the observer) describes to the rest of the group:

- How was Student 1's (counsellor's) body language, listening skills, questioning skills?
- Did the counsellor show sympathy and understanding?
- Did the counsellor get the counselled to think for him/herself or was the counsellor tempted to advise?
- How comfortable did the counselled student look? Was s/he put at ease?
- Did s/he explain the problem clearly?
- Was s/he convincing in the role?
- Had s/he prepared the problem to sufficient depth to allow worthwhile counselling to take place?
- Did you agree with student 1 and 2's accounts of the session?

Rotation 2: 1C, 2A, 3B

Student 2 now counsels Student 3. Student 1 observes.

Feedback 2

Discuss the points in Feedback 1.

Rotation 3: 1B, 2C, 3A

Student 3 now counsels Student 1. Student 2 observes.

Feedback 3

- Discuss the points in Feedback 1.
- Discuss any improvements on the first counselling session.

Optional Extra Session: Repeat the session using students' own problems, working in pairs.

Conclusion

All the groups reassemble to discuss what has been learnt from the feedback sessions.

- Do you feel more confident about the idea of seeking help?
- Do you feel more confident about giving help?
- Do you feel your skills have improved?

Problem Bank

Example of Counselling Problems (ages 15 to 16)

Most of these problems are intended for use by either sex.

Best friend

My best friend is being taken away from me, spending more and more time with someone else in the class and I feel left out and alone. And very jealous. I'm also too embarrassed to explain to my parents why s/he rarely phones or visits. What should I do?

Uncle

My uncle keeps visiting when my parents aren't home to check that I'm all right but he keeps touching my hands, face and hair unnecessarily and stands too close. He hasn't actually done anything I can complain about (except making me feel uncomfortable) so I can't tell my parents. They'd think I was making it up or that my mind was warping someone else's kindness into something nasty. I've got a younger sister too – will he do something to her if I don't stop it? I don't know what to do.

Teacher

Mrs X keeps picking on me for everything. She doesn't shout at others when they hand in their homework late or when they talk in class. She picks on me every time I open my mouth and even tells me off when it's been someone else who's made a noise. Parents' evening is coming up and I'm worried she'll say unfair things about me to my parents and then I'll be in big trouble.

Smell

People in my class keep making jokes when I'm around about body odour and they smell their armpits, pretending to check it isn't them who smell. They make fun of my hair too and say it's greasy and they hope they don't catch lice. My Mum doesn't let me wash my hair more than once a week – she says it's all it needs and I can only have a bath twice a week. She says deodorants aren't necessary if you wash under your arms every night but I can smell the difference by the time I've walked to school and the smell stays in my clothes.

Gay

Friends say I'm gay. I truly admire my teacher but my friends say I fancy him/her. I feel very confused about my sexuality and really don't know whether I fancy people of my own sex or not. I spend time mostly with my own sex and get very impatient and irritable with those of the opposite sex. My parents keep hinting that St Valentine's day is coming up and have asked if I'm going to send a card to anyone. I'm not going to. I'm sixteen years old.

Pregnant

I'm fifteen years old and think I might be pregnant. I had sex with a boy two weeks ago and my period hasn't come – it's two days late. What shall I do? Or: I'm sixteen years old and my girlfriend thinks she might be pregnant. Her period is two days late and we had sex two weeks ago. What should we do?

I'm too young to run a home

My Dad left us a long time ago and Mum's very ill and cannot leave the house or do any housework. We're too afraid to tell the authorities that we're not coping as we're afraid they'll split us up and then who'd look after Mum? I'm fifteen years old and I have to pick my younger brother up from school (and take him there in the mornings), I have to shop on my way home, cook our meals, do most of the housework and look after Mum. I'm either too tired to do homework or don't have the time. I'm too tired to concentrate in school as well. What should I do?

There's too many of us

I come from a big family and we live in a small house. The only place to work is at the dining table – the television is in the same through room and is on all the time, as my older brother and sister and my parents want to watch it. The whole house is noisy and I just cannot concentrate. My parents think I can work anywhere with any amount of noise but it's not true. What can I do?

I'm being threatened

A group of boys are threatening me for my pocket money which I've given them, but now they say they want more and are making me go into shops to steal for them. I'm scared I'll get caught.

Guarded toilets

There are a group of girls/boys who guard the toilets at break and don't let me in – so I can't go to the toilets at all – this is especially bad when I've got my period/ get diarrhoea as I have to go then. I often walk to another set of toilets at the opposite end of the school on the top floor, but that makes me late for lessons and often I get sent out by a teacher before I even get there, as I'm not supposed to be inside at break times.

Party failure

I'm new to the school and my Mum offered to give a party so that I could invite my new friends round to help me fit in better. The girls/boys that I'd invited were really friendly and promised they'd come, but on the day no one turned up and I felt dreadful knowing the trouble and expense that my Mum had gone to. Now she's worried about me too. Back at school, I was ignored by the people I'd invited and they just laughed at me behind my back. They'd done it on purpose! They hate me and I don't understand why.

I fancy someone

I really fancy someone but can't pluck up the courage to ask him/her out. I'm far too shy. How can I let him/her know I like him/her?

I miss my cat

My cat was put down last week because she was old and deaf. It was also because I didn't help out enough with looking after her and now I feel so guilty. Perhaps she would have gone on living for a long time if she'd been taken good care of. Now I miss her so much. I keep imagining that I can see her out of the corner of my eye and I keep looking down to check I won't step on her, but she's gone.

New baby

My Mum's just had another baby with a gap of fifteen years between us. I'm used to having my Mum all to myself but now she hardly has any time for me as the baby's always crying or needs to be fed or changed. Or I have to be quiet as the baby's just gone off to sleep. My Mum thought I'd be pleased to have a baby brother but I'm not. It would have been different when I was small as I could have played with him, but I've been an only child for fifteen years and now I feel I've got an intruder in the home.

Lost job

My Mum was made redundant a couple of months ago. My Dad's been unemployed for years so we really needed the money she earned to keep us going. Now I'm worried there won't be enough for us to eat and dread having to make an excuse for the school trip — how do I let people know we can't afford it? It's so humiliating. When I go out with my friends they've always got drink with them and I keep getting drunk trying to forget about my worries.

Mum's boyfriends

My Mum has had several boyfriends since my Dad left us three years ago. Boys in my class keep calling her a slag. I don't know what to do about it or how to protect my Mum. She's a good mother but I don't like her having so many boyfriends – I blame her for the aggro I'm getting at school. She's not really a slag, is she?

Remarried

My Dad's remarried. I can't understand how he could have forgotten my Mum so quickly – it was only two years ago that she died. I feel hurt and betrayed. I blame his new wife for forcing her way into our home and will never make friends with her. I want her out and I want my Dad back to myself.

Tidy room

I'm getting to school later and later each week. I can't leave the house until my room is tidy. Not just tidy as other people mean it, but really tidy. The curtains have to line up perfectly with the window frame. My bed mustn't have any creases in it. There can't be a speck of dust in the room or dirt on the carpet. My Mum can't understand it and I'm feeling frightened that I'm being taken over by this urge to sort my room out. I'm worried about it when I'm at school in case my Mum goes in there while I'm out and messes something up. It's taking me longer and longer to be happy with the state of my room – often I don't want to come to school at all as I want to guard the tidiness. What's wrong with me?

Problem Bank
Example of Counselling Problems
(ages 15 to 17)

Soap mad

I watch all the soaps on TV like Neighbours, Brookside, Home and Away, Eastenders, Heartbreak High, and I think about the characters all day. It's got so bad that my lessons are suffering. My homework only gets done after I've watched all my favourite soaps, but more and more often it just doesn't get done at all. My parents keep on at me for watching so much telly, but I won't let them switch it off. I think I'm addicted. What shall I do?

Buck teeth

I get called 'Goofy' and 'Rabbit Face' because my two front teeth stick out. They've been corrected but are still not perfect. I have such a low self-esteem over this that I'm feeling really depressed. I can't bear to go out unless I absolutely have to and keep wondering what people are saying about me. Now that two of my friends have boyfriends I feel even worse because I know nobody will want to go out with me.

Arranged marriage

My parents expect to choose my partner for me just as they were chosen by their parents. But I have been brought up in a different cultural environment and having seen how others live, I know that I want to have more control over my own life and to make such an important decision myself. Then if things go wrong I only have myself to blame — but there is a chance I might make the right choice. It is my life and I want to have a say in it. But how will I make them understand?

Divorce

My parents are getting a divorce and they keep arguing over who's going to have me live with them. They haven't even asked me for my opinion – but it means I'll be split up from my sister as they want to have a child each. I feel so helpless and out of control of my life.

Drugs

There are always Ecstasy tablets available at the parties I go to. So far I haven't tried one as I'm scared to – but now I'm the only one in my group who hasn't – the others take them regularly. Now they're forcing me to have one, offering to buy one for me as I'm so 'stingy'. If I don't take one, I'll risk losing my friends. If I do, I'll be scared out of my mind and I know that they wouldn't let me stop at just trying the one. My Mum's always warned me off drugs as she's a nurse and has seen what they do to people.

Drunk

My Mum's friend helps out at the youth club I go to. On Saturday there was a disco and we smuggled drink in through the girls' toilets. I got really drunk and kept being sick. It was my Mum's friend who looked after me. My Mum didn't know I got drunk because I stayed the night at a friend's house – but I'm worried her friend will tell her all about it.

Flick knife

My friend got this lethal looking flick knife for Christmas and since then he can't stop playing with it and running his finger up and down the blade, admiring how sharp it is. We're not allowed to bring knives to school/college but he never leaves his at home. I'm really worried he's going to use it on someone as he's started to use it in threats saying things like, 'D'you want your face carved up?'

Problem Bank
Example of Counselling Problems
(ages 16 to 19)

My partner's different

I have recently started going out with someone and my parents think that I'm out with my best friend but I'm not. My partner is of a completely different culture to me. I know that if my parents found out, they would forbid me to go out with this person again and would insist on their knowing all my friends so they can check up on me. But I hate lying to them – and the more lies I tell the more complicated everything gets.

I'm not allowed a boyfriend

A bloke I like asked me out but my parents won't let me see him out of college. When I asked them why they wouldn't say – just, 'You should know that by now'. I don't know what they think we would do – what's wrong with going to the cinema together or to the shops? I asked whether they trusted me or not and they said of course they did. But they don't and it makes me feel dirty. Also, what can I say to the bloke? He'll find someone else or won't believe that I like him.

My parents are homework mad

Every night my parents check my homework and if I haven't got any, they want to know why not. I'm not allowed to watch any television unless all my work has been done and they've examined my books. It's all they seem to be interested in. They never ask if I've had a good time at college, only what did I do in lessons. They expect me to get high marks in exams, but I find the work hard and never seem to come up to their expectations. If I do badly in an exam, they say it's because I haven't studied enough. I feel really miserable about life.

Overweight

I'm fat and wherever I go I hear people talking about me and laughing at me. I hate going to the shops now as I dread being stared at. I feel desperately unhappy. I've tried to diet, but I'm so miserable I often end up gorging myself on chocolate and cake, so it doesn't work.

Disasters

I have become very interested and worried about the possibility of a nuclear war or the world coming to an end from the greenhouse effect or from too much pollution. I just can't understand why we are all so wicked to one another and why other people can't see that we're heading towards destruction. It's virtually all I can think about and I'm feeling so depressed that there seems so little hope for the future. My life's not worth living if the world's going to end anyway. I feel so helpless that my future lies in the hands of other people.

Pretend boy/girlfriend

My friend makes up stories about a pretend partner. No one has ever met this partner and even his/her parents don't know – my friend says it's a secret. Should I tell him/her that I don't believe this person exists or should I put up with listening to all this make-believe?

Over-possessive

My boyfriend wants to know where I am every minute of the day. When I get up to go to the toilet he asks where am I going. If I need to go to my locker, he wants to come too. He's stifling me and I can't stand it. My friends have started making Siamese Twin jokes and saying he's my puppy dog. I don't want to hurt his feelings but if he doesn't stop I know I'll have to break off with him.

Drug-taking friend

I've just started at college and have made friends with a girl. She's the only one I'm going round with at the moment, but I've found out that she and her friends smoke pot. Will they expect me to join in too? When they go across the field to smoke I don't go with them. What should I do? I don't want to lose my only friend but I feel uncomfortable with her friends.

Casual sex

Recently I had sex with someone I met at a party. It was my first time and I didn't take any precautions. Also, I was drunk and didn't really know what I was doing. I know I'm not pregnant but I've started worrying more and more about whether I might have caught AIDS. I'm too scared to tell my parents as they would think I was a slut. What should I do?

Partner snatcher

Another person has a reputation for taking other people's partners. This person has recently started to hang around me and follow my partner, being very friendly. I'm worried that my partner will prefer this person to me – but how do I warn my partner without creating interest in this other person?

Lying boyfriend

My boyfriend told his friends that he'd slept with me which isn't true. But rumours have gone round about me and now people think I'm a bit of a 'goer' and that I'm easy. My reputation is ruined and people just don't believe me when I tell them it's not true – they think I'm just too embarrassed to admit it. Some of the girls have started to avoid me because of it – they think I'm bad news. How could he have done this to me?

Faddy eater

I've become very particular over what I eat. I've recently become a vegetarian but now I won't eat any dairy products either and I've cut out all sugary things. It makes it hard to eat out or be invited somewhere for a meal. My parents are mad at me because I'm so fussy and say I've lost too much weight. They're threatening to take me to the doctor. Why can't they see I just want to be healthy?

Lack of money

I've started work but I'm on a very low wage. My Mum expects me to pay for my keep now — something for my rent and something towards the food because she says I need to understand the value of money and since she's supported me up to now it's time I contributed to the household. It leaves me with just enough for my bus fares and a snack each day and for one night out a week. I'll need new clothes and shoes soon as I've got to look smart for work. My friends get to keep all their money and dress better than me.

Spendthrift

I've started work but never seem to have any money left before the next pay day. I spend everything I earn and never seem to have enough to get by. I'm earning more than I ever did when I had a Saturday job but I just can't save it or have enough for the whole month. I'm getting into debt because I've got several store cards and owe a lot already from shopping sprees.

Mean man

I've just moved in with my boyfriend but it's not what I expected. He has to know where I am every minute of the day. If I'm home late he thinks I'm with another bloke. Last night he hit me for the first time and I couldn't go into work because of the marks on my face. No one would believe I'd fallen downstairs or bumped into a door. My Mum's glad to have got me out of the house so I can't go back to her without a lot of begging. Besides, I don't think he'd let me he's that jealous — he thinks that now I'm there he owns me.

Unfaithful

I've been engaged to my girlfriend for a week now, but today I found out that she's been seeing someone else ever since we started going out together. She doesn't know I know about the other bloke. Now I think she only said yes to marrying me because she's pregnant. And with whose child? Can I trust her?

Suicidal

I want to kill myself because everything I've touched in life has gone wrong. I feel alienated from my family – no one cares about me or what I do. I haven't got any close friends, have never had a partner or anyone to talk over problems with. I'm unlovable and no one likes me. I may as well be dead.

Pressured

My girlfriend wants to move in with me and keeps making hints, but I don't feel we know each other well enough and I'm not prepared to make the commitment yet. She's miserable at home and her family argue so she might just be using me as an escape route. I don't want to rush into anything and I want to be sure it's right before we live together. She's quite hot-headed so I'm worried that if I tell her how I feel she'll dump me.

Lack of privacy

I share a flat with a friend. However, she's been getting more and more nosy, wanting to know everything I do and she listens to my telephone conversations. Yesterday I caught her in my room reading my diary and before this, a couple of my personal letters looked as though they'd been tampered with. I haven't got any privacy. It's like I'm being spied on.

Married man

I've been seeing a married man who told me that he and his wife no longer sleep together and are planning to get a divorce. By accident I saw his wife in a shop with a friend and only knew who she was because she gave the sales assistant her name as she was applying for a store card. She's absolutely stunning plus she was buying maternity clothes. I feel completely betrayed but can't help loving him.

Ill health

I've had a lot of pain and swelling in my joints that's been getting worse over the months. It's so bad that it's painful to walk and I'm off sick. I've just been diagnosed as having rheumatoid arthritis. It's a big blow and I wonder what I'm going to do – to be sick this early in life when my life's barely begun is something I can't cope with.

Chronic fatigue syndrome

I've had chronic fatigue syndrome (formerly known as ME) for two years now and there's no sign of improvement. I'm so tired that I can't leave the house. I even get tired talking for long and my muscles hurt too much to even hold a book to read. I've lost all my friends because I'm no fun and I'm desperately lonely. I feel as though my life is not worth living. It's not as though someone can wave a magic wand and say that I'll be better in six months. Some people never get better. And I'm a burden to my parents. They are getting old and tired themselves and have enough troubles already, without the added problem of having to look after me. I'd prefer to be dead.

Unfit

After leaving school I never did any sports and didn't do anything physical. Now I know I'm really unfit as I was invited to go swimming with a friend from work. I was really embarrassed to be so out of breath after swimming only a short distance and I know she thought I was a plonker. I'd like to do something about it, but I'm too embarrassed to join a gym or fitness club as I think everyone will laugh at me when I can't do things. But I don't want to go with anyone else either as they'll spread it around that I'm a flabby couch potato.

Termination

About a year and a half ago I had my pregnancy terminated. My boyfriend had left me and I was too afraid to tell my parents plus I didn't think I could cope bringing up a baby by myself. Now I'm haunted by baby adverts and keep seeing babies in the supermarket. I can't stop thinking that my child would have been about one now and I wish I'd had it after all. What makes it worse is that my boyfriend's come back and says he'd made a terrible mistake by leaving me and that he wants us back together. I don't know how I feel about him anymore. Last year I would have jumped at the chance.

I feel small

I had my baby when I was seventeen. She's now two and goes to nursery. The other mums are much older and I dread seeing them. Many of them get together for coffee mornings – I was invited to go along once but I hated it. They were all married and relatively well off, whereas I'm a single mum on benefit. I felt they looked down on me because I hadn't got a job, a partner or a nice home – I live in a high rise council flat. I know they were being snobbish but I judge myself harshly. I know I'm a fool and could have done better for myself. I don't fit in well with other single mums either because I came from a middle-class background and talk differently – they seem to resent it, or at least I don't feel comfortable with them nor they with me. I seem to be caught in between two worlds on my own. My mum won't have anything to do with me either as she thinks I've let her down.

Dodgy landlord

When I moved into the studio flat, my landlord made promises about seeing to the damp and mending the dripping taps and other jobs that needed attention. However, he now just waves his hand at me when I remind him of these things and obviously has no intention of putting it right. There's a gas fire and cooker that look suspect and I know he's supposed to get them inspected each year. But if I report him I might be left without a home.

Rape

I was raped two years ago on a date. I didn't tell anyone because I felt bad about it and thought I might be blamed for what happened. But now I've met someone I really like and I feel, for the first time since I was raped, that I might be able to trust him. He asked me out and I went, but I was terrified of him touching me. When he did hold my hand I pulled it away. He thinks I don't like him, but really it's just that I'm afraid of being touched. I'm scared of letting myself be physically dominated again. I know logically that I'd probably be safe, but the images of what happened before come back to haunt me.

STD

I've caught some sort of sexually transmitted disease. I've got bad pains low down and an unusual discharge. I slept with someone other than my partner for one night and think I must have caught it off him/her. I don't want to tell my partner about it, so have been making excuses as to why I don't want sex. I'm too ashamed to go to my family doctor.

Conclusion

Reasons for not giving advice (or telling the person who needs help) what to do are:

1. The person is an individual who knows themselves better than anyone else.

2. The person has had different life experiences to the counsellor and their personality/character is different too, so only they can decide what is appropriate for them.

3. Individuals know what they really want and orientate their behaviour to satisfy their perceived needs.

4. Individuals have the resources within them to achieve what they want.

National Helplines

National AIDS Helpline: 0800 567 123 (Free)

Albany Trust (Sexual Identity counselling): 0181 767 1827 (London)

Alcoholics Anonymous Helpline: 0171 833 0022 (London)

British Association for Counselling: 01788 578328 (Rugby)

British Pregnancy Advisory Service (Helpline): 01564 793225 (West Midlands)

Childline (24 hour): 0800 1111 (Free)

Cruse Bereavement Care: 0181 940 4818 (London)

Drinkline National Alcohol Helpline: 0345 32 02 02 (Local rate)

Eating Disorders Association (Anorexia/Bulimia): 01603 62 14 14 (Norwich); Youth Helpline: 01603 765050 (Norwich)

Family Planning Association Helpline: 0171 837 4044 (London) **Switchboard** 0171 837 5432

Lesbian and Gay Switchboard (24 hour): 0171 837 7324 (London)

Lifeline: Help for Victims of Violence in the Home: 01335 370825 (Support and advice for psychological, physical or sexual abuse)

MIND (National Association for Mental Health): 0181 519 2122 (London)

MIND information and advice line: 0181 522 1728 (London) 0345 660 163 (Local rate) (Including anorexia, bulimia, anxiety, bereavement, depression, phobias and obsessions, post-traumatic stress disorder, schizophrenia, seasonal affected disorder, suicide)

National Phobics Society: 0161 227 9898 (Manchester) Or write to: 4, Cheltenham Road, Manchester, M21 9QN (Phobias, panic attacks, obsessive compulsive disorder)

NSPCC (Child protection helpline; 24 hour): 0800 800 500 (Free)

Quitline (Smoking 9am–9pm, 7 days a week): 0171 487 3000 (London)

Rape Crisis (Rape/Sexual abuse; 24 hours): 0171 837 1600 (London)

Samaritans (General counselling, especially suicide): 0345 90 90 90 (Local rate) (e.g., loneliness, bullying, depression, sexual identity problems, suicide)

Samaritans (Head Office): 01753 53 27 13 (Berks)

SANELINE (Information and support): 0345 678 000 (Local Rate) (2pm-midnight every day)

Victim Support (National Office): 0171 735 9166 (London)

Women Against Sexual Harassment: 0171 405 0430 (London)

Bibliography

Alman, B.M and Lambrou, P. (1993) *Self-Hypnosis*. London: Souvenir Press Ltd.

Amos, J.A. (1996) *Managing Yourself*. Plymouth: How To Books Ltd.

Argyle, M. and Henderson, M. (1985) *The Anatomy of Relationships*. Pelican Books.

Argyle, M. and Trower, P. (1979) *Person to Person Ways of Communicating*. New York: Harper & Row Ltd.

Carnegie, D. (1953) *How to Win Friends and Influence People*. London: World's Work Ltd.

Cotterell, J. (1996) *Social Networks and Social Influences in Adolescence*. London: Routledge.

Csóti, M. (1997) *Assertiveness Skills for Young Adults*. Peterborough: First and Best in Education Ltd.

Eggert, M. (1996) *Perfect Counselling*. London: Arrow Books Ltd.

Fensterheim, H. and Baer, J. (1976) *Don't Say 'Yes' When You Want To Say 'No'*. London: Futura Publications.

Gibbs, A. (1986) *Understanding Mental Health*. London: Consumer's Association.

Hargie, O., Saunders, C. and Dickson, D. (1994) *Social Skills in Interpersonal Communication*. London: Routledge.

Hartley, P. (1993) *Interpersonal Communication*. London: Routledge.

Nelson Jones, R. (1991) *Human Relationship Skills, Second Edition*. London: Cassell Plc.

Shelton, N. and Burton, S. (1994) *Assertiveness Skills*. London: Richard D. Irwin, Inc.

Shapiro, M. (1993) *Successful Interviewing in a Week*. London: Hodder and Stoughton Ltd.

Varah, C. (1985) *The Samaritans Befriending the Suicidal*. London: Constable and Company Limited.

Printed in the United Kingdom
by Lightning Source UK Ltd.
113804UKS00001B/53-70